C000259783

The Nonviolent Radical

The Nonviolent Radical

Seeing and Living the Wisdom of Jesus

Charles McCollough

WIPF & STOCK · Eugene, Oregon

THE NONVIOLENT RADICAL
Seeing and Living the Wisdom of Jesus

Copyright © 2012 Charles McCollough. All rights reserved. Except for brief quotations in critical publications or reviews, no part of this book may be reproduced in any manner without prior written permission from the publisher. Write: Permissions, Wipf and Stock Publishers, 199 W. 8th Ave., Suite 3, Eugene, OR 97401.

Wipf and Stock
An imprint of Wipf and Stock Publishers
199 W. 8th Ave., Suite 3
Eugene, OR 97401
www.wipfandstock.com

ISBN 13: 978-1-60899-965-1

New Revised Standard Version Bible, copyright 1989, Division of Christian Education of the National Council of the Churches of Christ in the United States of America. Used by permission. All rights reserved.

To Carol

"What is art supposed to do except make us say, Wow!—to strip the skin of dullness from what we see?"

—John Updike

"You use a glass mirror to see your face. You use works of art to see your soul."

—George Bernard Shaw

". . . indigenous people have much insight to offer to those who seem to have garnered the best seats for themselves at the Lord's Table."

—The Rev. Rosemary McCombs Maxey, Mvskoke/Creek

"Europeans . . . believed the whole Indian way of life was the work of the devil and the powers of evil, wickedness, and ignorance . . . and we believed them and gave it up—gave the whole thing up. And then what did Christianity do? Turn around and replace our superstitions with a set of their own."

—The Rev. Vine V. Deloria, Sr., Standing Rock Sioux

Contents

Illustrations

Foreword

IN THE BEGINNING THE Spirit blew over the depths of Charles McCollough's heart: "Let my word spring forth in clay, as sculpted images of the wisdom of the logos, of the living Christ." Then, through years of thinking and studying the wisdom of Christ and molding clay with his hands, the artist-theologian produced an astounding number of clay relief sculptures that give material, visual embodiment to the wisdom sayings of Jesus. In some cases Christ's sharp meanings had been smoothed and worn away by spiritualizing them, avoiding how they engaged the powers and principalities of the Roman Empire. By reading Christ's sayings in the context of political oppression, and by offering us striking, dramatic images of them, McCollough makes the familiar words of Christ cut to the marrow of our being.

The earthen texture of the sculptures reinforces the author-artist's insistence that we not spiritualize Jesus' wisdom teachings when he is in fact talking about physical impoverishment and brutal inequality. The art incarnates the truth that McCollough describes in his prose, compelling us to see the meaning of the gospel in the context of the injustice and oppression that characterize our world every bit as much as they did the Roman Empire.

McCollough's reliefs make me think of reliefs I have seen in archeological publications and art museums featuring work from the ancient near east, but updated with a sensibility in tune with our own period of history. While maintaining that contemporary style, McCollough sometimes pictures a saying of Jesus in the context of New Testament times. I think, for example, of his sculpture of three Roman centurions cowering over a victim lying face down on the ground with his hands tied behind his back. We shudder with the terror the text awakens: "Wherever the corpse is, there the vultures [eagles] will gather." But McCollough is not content to leave things in the past. He also pictures the overthrow of the high and mighty that Mary celebrates in the Magnificat by picturing a brave woman standing with an empty hand raised in opposition to an on coming tank. In a set of two panels on the beatitude, "Blessed are the persecuted," McCollough portrays the terror of regimes that compel children to serve in the military. In one sculpture a teenage boy sits in despair next to his automatic weapon, and then, in a contrasting image, the weapon is tied to a tree while the boy stands lifting up his arms in joy, completely freed from the encumbrance of the gun.

To see tanks and guns as well as Roman swords and armor portrayed through the ancient medium of clay relief sculptures is to sense interconnections that reach across the centuries, interconnections of social inequality and military violence, but also our interconnection with the spirit of Christ who works to topple oppression throughout the ages. McCollough's prose and art complement one another to bring Christ's wisdom urgently alive.

I can personally attest to how helpful this book is to receiving anew the wisdom of Christ. A few years ago I had the privilege of leading a week-long homiletics conference with Charles McCollough. Our theme was the beatitudes of Christ, and our worship space was adorned with many of the sculptures featured in this book. Each participant had to choose one beatitude-inspired sculpture and use it in a sermon. The sermons were among the best I have heard on the beatitudes. McCollough's art had awakened insight and fresh language in the preachers. We received the parables as though we had just heard them directly from Christ.

In relating this experience I do not mean to imply the book is for preachers only. It is not. McCollough's book is for anyone who wants to receive more fully and keenly the wisdom sayings of Christ.

McCollough has composed a duet for two voices. One voice is his lucid and revealing interpretation of well-known biblical passages. The other voice is his visual art. Like any duet, it is possible to sing just one part and get a partial idea of what the composer intended. But the only way to appreciate fully the composition is to listen to both parts. I found myself holding the photographs of the sculptures before me as I read the sayings of Jesus and McCollough's interpretation of them. Again and again I was struck how the "word" of God is so much more than purely language. Yes, the word is expressed through concept, thought, and speech, but it also finds articulation in mud, in clay, in the materiality of the created word that is shaped into new visions by an artist as imaginative, gifted, and faithful as Charles McCollough.

Thomas H. Troeger
Professor of Christian Communication
Yale Divinity School and Institute of Sacred Music

Acknowledgments

I HAVE THREE GROUPS of friends to acknowledge for helping me with this book and DVD: scholars whose books are listed in the bibliography, artists and art teachers, and personal and professional friends.

I am indebted to the scholars who have applied the tools of historical criticism to Scripture and history, but I also include the voices of the formally colonized people. The term "Postcolonial" is a label for these scholars and Bible readers. I have learned much from native people who were colonized by the United States and who still struggle to free Christianity from its abuse as a tool of western domination. Especially helpful have been the native people of the northern plains, the Eagle Butte Learning Center, Rosemary McCombs Maxey of the Mvskoke Nation, and the native people of Hawai'i, particularly Kekapa Lee, Napua and Kini Burke, Kaleo Patterson, Auntie Verdelle Lum, and Randy Furushima.

Alyce McKenzie of Perkins School of Theology got me started on Jesus' proverbs, and Warren Carter of Brite Divinity School was especially helpful to me with his work on the Roman context of the New Testament. Thomas Troeger of Yale Divinity School helped me with his imaginative poetry, art appreciation, and music. I am especially grateful for his Foreword to this book. Gregg Mast, Rene House, Richard Strum, and Tim Mulder at New Brunswick Theological Seminary all supported my work there with a number of commissions and teaching opportunities.

My art teachers, John Carbone and the late Jim Colavita, gave many years of helpful critique of my sculpture, and the classical sculptural works of Pheidias, Tilman Riemenschneider, Michaelangelo Buonarroti, Käthe Kolwitz, Ernst Barlach, and Giacomo Manz'u still inspire me. Painters Rembrandt Harmensz van Rijn, Francisco Goya, Vincent Van Gogh, as well as living artists Rein Poortvliet from Holland and Sergio Toppi from Italy also influenced my sculpture.

Personal and professional friends have been essential to this project, namely: Martie McMane of Boulder, CO; Jeffrey Mays of Princeton, NJ; Heather Elkins and Danna Nolan Fewell of Drew Theological School; and the late Ursula Kaplowitz. My editor, Ulrike Guthrie, also a fine painter, did careful work on the text for which I am grateful. Doug Purnell, artist and theologian, is always helpful.

Most of all I am grateful for the constant support of my life partner and wife, Carol K. McCollough. She has given endless hours of crucial work to this project, especially to the DVD and its technical challenges.

All of the stories in the book are real experiences, but I have disguised names and contexts in most, but not all, stories to avoid embarrassing friends and myself.

1

Introduction to *The Nonviolent Radical: Seeing and Living the Wisdom of Jesus*

> She was stuck in New York City traffic on the way to a party wondering if she was dressed properly. "A blustery March wind whipped the steam coming out of the manholes, and people hurried along the sidewalks with their collars turned up." She looked out the car window to see a woman rooting through a dumpster. That dumpster diver was her mother.

So begins Jeannette Walls' best-selling memoir, *The Glass Castle*.[1] Her discovery of her mother in the dumpster shocks us, but less so after we learn of Walls' childhood years of extreme poverty, an alcoholic and violent father, a negligent mother who did not protect Jeannette, her siblings or herself, and years of what most people would call "child abuse." Yet Walls seems to have thrived as a child, graduated from college, and is now a successful writer.

What is truly shocking and almost unbelievable is how Walls could write a book all about her growing up in such a degrading environment without the slightest hint of judgment or blame of her parents or anyone else, only a lovingly kind book about a woman who followed the wisdom: *Do not judge.*

We all live our daily lives following the stated and assumed wisdom of the past. If we are Christians, we try to live by, teach, and preach the wisdom of Jesus each day and most deliberately on Sundays. For example, Jesus is quoted as saying: "Do not judge, so that you may not

1. Walls, *The Glass Castle*, 3.

be judged. For with the judgment you make you will be judged, and the measure you give will be the measure you get. Why do you see the speck in your neighbor's eye, but do not notice the log in your own eye?" (Matt 7:1–3; Luke 6:36–38).

We know from psychology that though judging and blaming others may be an entertaining habit, it is usually useless and often makes matters worse. On a personal level, psychological counseling succeeds only when the patient feels he or she is not being judged or blamed.

The same applies on interpersonal and social levels. Marriage counseling begins with the wisdom of Do Not Blame. And management-labor mediation and international diplomacy cannot work if one side insists on the other's exclusive fault. Judging and blaming on all levels is counterproductive, and Jesus preached this already over two thousand years ago.

But we still don't get it; judging and blaming are too much fun. Maybe a picture can communicate when words do not.

Judge Not

This image of a sculpture shows an aggressive man seeking to remove a speck from the eye of a hapless soul who, in turn, tries unsuccessfully to push away his blaming hand and to point out the beam in the blamer's eye.

WHAT THIS BOOK IS ABOUT

This book seeks to do three things:

1. To show with images as well as to tell with words the meaning of wisdom sayings attributed to Jesus;
2. To interpret those wisdom sayings in the context of the economic and political world in which they were spoken; and
3. To provide practical ways to teach, preach, and live that wisdom today on both a private and a public level with both words and images.

I will assume the scholarly study of the gospels and the details of historical, form, textual, redactive, source, reader response, and postcolonial criticism, but I will keep that in the background. For I am aware that people today, and especially the young, obtain and maintain their wisdom in concise doses and with visual images. So you may use my images in this book[2] for teaching, preaching, and daily living.[3] My goal is to help us *see* with images the wisdom of Jesus.

I do not include the wisdom of Jesus' parables in this book because they are available in my previous book, *The Art of Parables*, published by Wood Lake Publishing Inc., 2008. I learned from doing presentations on that parable book how eager people are to have images of biblical words and how eye-opening are the Bible's economic and political perspectives. For although we tend to view the Bible almost exclusively from a private, personal level and ignore the economy and politics of the first century and our own, in fact the economy and politics cut deeply into our daily lives and attention to them illuminates the Bible's often strange teachings. For example, when we read that Jesus was called *the* "Son of God," it makes a big difference to know that Caesar was also called *the* "Son of God," or that Herod was supposed to be the "King of the Jews" while his

2. A DVD with many more images could not be included in this book but is available from the author. Send $12.00 plus postage to C. McCollough, 165 Hopewell-Wertsville, Rd Hopewell, NJ 08525.

3. I grant permission for use of these images from the book and DVD for educational purposes as long as I am credited for the images and no sale is made of them. Kindly send me copies of such use at cmccollough2@verizon.net.

disciples called Jesus that same name. One scholar calls such naming of Jesus, "high treason."[4] Why is this clearly political matter of calling Jesus political names almost always avoided in favor of a spiritualized claim that Jesus was God, a name that a number of the Roman emperors also claimed for themselves?

To be sure, a recent rash of scholarly books has emphasized empire, peasant, subaltern, and political studies in the use and abuse of the Bible. But who in our pews or even our pulpits really reads these books or thinks from more than the radical, individualistic perspective of modern, western thought? I have read most of these books and delight in such visual resources as *Living the Questions* (LTQ), which I have used in my church. Virtually all of the scholars in that series include fine analysis of political/economic issues in Jesus' life. Yet even so they are essentially talking heads. By contrast, in this book I seek to interpret Jesus' wisdom sayings with original, visual art. My interpretation recognizes the interconnectedness of the economy, politics, and religion in the Bible for there was no separation of these areas in Biblical times. Unlike our modern separation of church and state, no such separation existed in biblical times.

Now a brief overview of *wisdom* in the Bible:

Wisdom is a very broad and even a cosmic and apocalyptic concept. It is the translation of *Logos,* and it is expressed in a literary form called a *māšāl* in the First Testament. The *māšāl* includes proverbs, parables, sayings, allegories, maxims, aphorisms, figures of speech, and similitudes. Most often in this book I will refer to proverbs. Alyce McKenzie helpfully defines a proverb as: "a short saying that expresses a complete thought, which, while most often expressing traditional values, is also capable of subverting them, offering ethical directives in certain new situations that are most often implied rather than directly stated."[5] Or, more simply, "a short sentence founded upon long experience, containing a truth."[6]

My approach is twofold: I will use visual art to express my interpretations of Jesus' wisdom and I will interpret that wisdom in the political and economic context of his time. Jesus' context was life in a colony

4. Crossan, *God and Empire*, 141.

5. McKenzie, *Preaching Proverbs*, 3.

6. Attributed to Cervantes, in McKenzie, *Preaching Proverbs*, xv.

of Rome in which 95 to 97 percent[7] of the people were ruthlessly exploited in order to support the conspicuous consumption of the 3 to 5 percent elite in what scholars call an "aristocratic empire." Jesus did not ignore the way this empire dominated 95 percent of the people with violence, fear, and state terror. Indeed, his central message and behavior proclaimed the opposite empire of nonviolence, courage, love, and the Empire of God that is in direct conflict with the Empire of Rome.

This economic and political approach goes against centuries of popular and scholarly study of the Bible, which has typically spiritualized, privatized, and individualized the text. Not only has the Bible been interpreted through these privatized eyes, the Bible itself also contains in some places justifications for imperial domination claiming it to be God's will in spite of the teachings of the prophets and Jesus. But, as notes R.S. Sugirtharajah, postcolonial scholar and Professor of Biblical Hermeneutics at the University of Birmingham, there has been a "remarkable reluctance among biblical scholars to speak of imperialism in shaping the contours of biblical texts and their interpretation."[8]

Musa W. Dube of the University of Botswana spells out this approach of former colonial countries as follows: "Decolonizing defines [1.] awareness of imperialism's exploitative forces and its various strategies of domination, [2.] the conscious adoption of strategies of resisting imperial domination, as well as [3.] the search for alternative ways of liberating interdependence between nations, races, genders, economies and cultures."[9]

Postcolonial theology focuses especially on how the Bible has been used to promote this imperialism and even includes imperial, i.e. colonizing, messages itself in the text. Dube, for example, shows how John 4, in which Jesus converts the Samaritan woman and other Samaritans, is used as such an imperial text.[10] This passage is later used to justify proselytizing non-Christians.

In the last three centuries northern nations have colonized almost all of the southern lands. Most western, Christian churches saw this

7. These percentages are flexible, of course. I will use the 95 percent and 5 percent numbers here.

8. Sugirtharajah, *Postcolonial Criticism and Biblical Interpretation*, 74.

9. Dube, "Reading for Decolonization (John 4:1–42)" in Dube and Staley, *John and Postcolonialism*, 52 (my numbers).

10. Ibid., 51–75.

imperial conquest of the rest of the world as an opportunity and even a duty to evangelize, Christianize, and civilize the "heathen." The results are shameful. While such conquest brought Christianity and some helpful benefits to the colonized world, the upheaval, new diseases, and economic and political oppression dominated to such an extent that some even call this colonization a "holocaust" and current policies of globalization "neo-colonialism."

Now the people of Africa, Asia, the Pacific Islands, South and Central America, as well as descendents of former slaves and native people are pushing back and calling for a new look at the Bible, one that does not justify imperial conquest. They use new tools of interpretation to apply Jesus' anti-imperial wisdom to our own context and time.

IN THREE PARTS

This book is in three parts. The reasons for these divisions are simple: Part 1 covers the wisdom sayings about blessings in the Magnificat and the Beatitudes in Jesus' time and our own. These brief summarizations in the gospels need to be unpacked and spelled out separately from Jesus' other sayings. They are tight condensations of God's blessings that urge us to draw out their meaning for us today. Part 2 deals with Jesus' wisdom on nonviolence which is so misunderstood and misused today that we need to give special attention to its meaning and implications. Part 3 focuses on a number of daily life issues that have perplexed people through the ages and that I reinterpret for us today.

In spite of my divisions of Jesus' wisdom sayings, they are of course interrelated, and the separation here is only for convenience to help us decipher their meanings.

Avoiding False Assumptions Where Possible.

It is easy and, even natural, to enter the first-century texts with our twenty-first century assumptions. Some of these assumptions are false, such as:

- That Jesus' wisdom was for individuals alone. This false assumption is natural for us because of our extreme individualism that is repeatedly documented by scholars. However, much of the world today and all of it in Jesus' time assumed an extended family, tribal, and corporate identity.

- That Jesus' wisdom assumed a separation of religion and politics. Although we assume a separation of church and state in the U.S., there was no such thing in the first century. The Caesars were not only political/state leaders, but many were also high priests and even called "god." Jesus was not only a private religious leader; he also resisted political oppression, and did so nonviolently.
- That Jesus was non-resistant. Jesus was nonviolent but he was not non-resistant. He resisted evil, Rome, and Rome's appointed authorities. He rejected the violence of the Zealots but was never passive. He aggressively challenged the "hypocrites" and condemned whole cities such as Chorazin, Bethsaida, Tyre, Sidon, and Capernaum (Matt 11:20–23).
- That Jesus sought to break with Judaism and start a new religion. On the contrary, even though Jesus opposed the Rome-appointed priests and other collaborators, he still sought to fulfill the Mosaic law and the prophets of Judaism (Matt 5:17).

Although I will seek to avoid these assumptions, it is impossible finally to avoid my own historic and social location and to pretend objectivity. I have the privileges of a white, western male and cannot erase them. However, I can hear, see, and affirm those who do not have my history and location and have suffered the imperialism of those of us who have been so privileged. However, I have also been blessed with frequent and profound relationships with native and other non-western people who have taught me how limited some western ideas and assumptions are and how wise and Christ-like some of these non-western views can be. One such limited western assumption is that Rome's power was benign, even glorious. Quite the contrary! Rome ruled with extreme violence and state terror. Here I briefly summarize Rome's power over its colonies as the context of the wisdom of Jesus, noting my indebtedness to scholars such as Warren Carter, Richard Horsley. R.S. Sugirtharajah, Sharon Ringe, Musa Dube, and John Dominic Crossan for their writings on the biblical context of the economy and politics of the first century, and to James C. Scott, John H. Kautsky, and Paul Zanker for their historical, political, and artistic perspectives on Roman and other aristocratic empires.

It is helpful to have a general summary of the economic and political context of Jesus' wisdom sayings in order to understand them. This will only be only a brief sketch because I will expand on this context as I interpret each saying. Also, this book's bibliography refers to many more thorough descriptions of the economy and the political realities of Jesus' time.

WHAT THIS BOOK IS NOT

I intend this book to be a very practical application of the wisdom of the historical Jesus on specific life questions about which we must frequently think, speak, and decide, questions like: What does God bless? What does Jesus teach about violence? What would Jesus do about the many daily problems we face?

What this book does not deal with is the incarnation of Christ as the *Logos*, Wisdom, Word, and Sophia of God—that is, the church's post-Easter understanding of the risen Christ. The many recent books on the Sophia of God manifested in Jesus Christ help correct the patriarchal bias of the Bible and theology through the ages. The emphasis on Sophia, a sacred feminine aspect of God, wisely helps balance this male prejudice and opens a broader, more compassionate metaphor of God.

A very readable summary of both the wisdom of the historical Jesus and of Christ, the Sophia of God, is Marcus Borg's *Meeting Jesus Again for the First Time.*[11] One chapter (4) is on the historical Jesus as a teacher of wisdom. Another (5) is on Christ as the *Logos*, Wisdom, Word, and Sophia of God. Borg says that Jesus as a wisdom teacher "used aphorisms and parables to invite his hearers to *see* in a radically new way. The appeal is to the imagination, to that place within us in which reside our images of reality and our images of life itself; the invitation is to a different way of seeing."[12]

My special concern is to go beyond words to *see* with a "transformation of our perception" (which Borg sees as "the best explanation of the origin of Jesus' wisdom."[13]) by creating sculptural images of Jesus' wisdom sayings in parables, aphorisms, and proverbs.

HOW TO USE THIS BOOK AND DVD[14]

Settings: The DVD can be used in worship or in educational settings.

11. Borg, *Meeting Jesus Again*, 69–118.

12. Ibid., 74.

13. Ibid., 87.

14. The DVD It is available from the author at 165 Hopewell-Wertsville Rd.,

Duration options: One time use, six weeks, or year long series studying one or two sayings per session

Timing for educational setting: 75 minutes (total)

Equipment needed for DVD use: Computer, Multimedia projector, screen, room with muted light

Use of equipment: The DVD can be downloaded to your computer hard drive and then paused to focus on each wisdom saying. The images are to be studied as well as the texts.

Leadership: If a biblical expert is unavailable, members can take turns leading each session. Such leaders can read the chapter to be considered two or three time and ask the participants to discuss the questions below. No need to lecture or assume expertise.

Some discussion questions:

1. What is the economic and political context of the wisdom saying?
2. If there is more than one version of the saying in the different gospels, compare them and consider the meaning of the differences.
3. How does the author's view differ or concur with your or the usual view of the saying?
4. How does Jesus' wisdom saying apply to you on a personal and public level?
5. How should the church apply the wisdom of Jesus' sayings? Is the church fulfilling that wisdom, or does it need to change? How?

A sample schedule for education sessions of 75 minutes each:

- 5 minutes for gathering and opening prayer (More time can be allowed the first session for introductions and making name tags.)
- 10 minutes to read aloud the saying, including the context before and after the saying
- 25 minutes to discuss the meaning of the saying
- 10 minutes to project the images of the saying
- 15 minutes to discuss the images of the saying
- 10 minutes for ending prayer and assignment
- 75 minutes

Note: When showing the full DVD, music is helpful.

Hopewell, NJ 08525. Send $12.00 plus postage.

2

The Colonial Context of Jesus' Wisdom

UNDERSTANDING ROME

JESUS' WORLD WAS ONE overwhelmingly dominated by the Roman Empire. Rome must be seen in the foreground when we read the New Testament and not the background, as Warren Carter points out.[1] Indeed, "without understanding the Roman imperial world, we will find it hard to understand the New Testament texts."[2] For example, just by reading the Christmas story or seeing the traditional Christmas pageant in our churches, we learn that Mary and Joseph had to go to Bethlehem to be registered because Caesar Augustus had declared a census. Many of us modern readers are unaware of why this census occurred. The census was taken so that Caesar could tax and demand tribute from everyone in the lands Rome had conquered. This was the price colonies usually paid to their conquering overlords to "be protected," much as criminal gangs "protect" those they dominate nowadays. Such payments were used for roads, aqueducts, theaters, temples, and baths built with involuntary labor, but especially for military forces to implement Rome's plans for further conquests of more lands and peoples.

Land was the main commercial base for this agrarian society. Land determined wealth for the 5 percent who were rich as well as the survival of the 95 percent who were poor. Refusal to pay taxes and tribute was considered treasonous and was countered with extreme violence and intimidation. When Herod died in 4 CE, Jewish rebels tried to throw off the tyranny of Rome and the prospect of any other vicious puppet king

1. Carter, *The Roman Empire and the New Testament*, ix.

2. Ibid., 2–3.

like Herod that Rome would install. But the Roman military ruthlessly crushed this effort and crucified hundreds of the suspected rebels. Their bodies were left to rot on poles and crosses in order to terrorize and intimidate anyone who dared oppose the Roman system and its local supporters. Growing up, Jesus would have known of such violence and was careful to resist the local Roman collaborators using nonviolent means. He tried to heal and feed the traumatized victims of this state terrorism.

Peasants were taxed at extortionate levels, (estimates vary wildly between 30 percent and 70 percent) and were losing their land, their source of survival, because they had to borrow money to pay taxes, rents, tributes, and tolls, not to mention the tithes to the temple, using their land as collateral. When they could not pay, their land was taken. It often was joined to other land to form large plantations to grow cash crops for export, leaving the peasants with no way to survive except as tenant farmers, day laborers, beggars, prostitutes, or bandits. These conditions are laid out in parables such as the ones about the "Wicked Tenants" (Matt 21:33–41), "The Talents" (Matt 25:14–30), the "Vineyard Workers" (Matt 20:1–16), and "The Doorkeepers and Overseer" (Matt 24:45–51). These parables give examples of absentee landlords who expected slaves and servants (often peasants who had lost their land) to keep the landlords' plantations profitable and in good order.

With 95 percent supporting the few elites, there was no middle class. The system was rigged for the rich to get richer and the poor to get poorer. This is likely what Jesus meant when he analyzed the economy saying, "To those who have, more will be given; and from those who do not have, even what they seem to have will be taken away" (Luke 8:18b).

PRAYER AS TREASON

The tiny elite served themselves and appeased their Roman overlords by extorting the taxes, tributes, rents, tolls, and temple tithes, and by keeping the so-called Roman peace—which meant no opposition was tolerated. Yet, when Jesus prayed, "Our father," he was referring not to Caesar but to the God of Moses and the prophets. And "thy kingdom come" did not mean domination by "Eternal Rome" but peace and justice of God's Kingdom. "Forgive us our debts as we forgive others," would wreck the system of land seizure for commercialization of agriculture. "For yours is the kingdom, power and glory" was not for the emperor, the "Senate and the People of Rome" (SPQR, one of Rome's symbols) or for the vaunted military, but for the God of shalom for all people. So even the Lord's Prayer, seen in the context of the realities of Roman tyranny, was seditious propaganda.[3] Thus Jesus was murdered by Roman decree.

How can anyone ignore this political and economic context of Jesus' world? Yet, for two thousand years that has been the most common way to read the wisdom of Jesus. Clearly we must understand Rome in order to understand the New Testament. And we must also be aware of the economic and political realities of Jesus' time to decipher the coded messages in his wisdom.

By "coded" I refer to the "hidden transcript" as opposed to the "public transcript." James C. Scott, social scientist at Yale, has extensively studied these coded expressions by subordinate groups (the 95 percent in Jesus' time). The hidden transcript is "the veiled cultural struggle and political expression of subordinate groups who have ample reason to fear venturing their unguarded opinion." [4] "The meaning of the text . . . is rarely straight-forward: it is often meant to communicate one thing to those in the know and another to outsiders and authorities."[5] Thus, Richard A. Horsley in his 2008 book, *Jesus in Context*, writes, "We are just beginning to explore how Jesus traditions can be understood as rooted in a Galilean Israelite "hidden transcript."[6] What if the gospels are indeed codes with hidden meanings familiar to Jewish peasants but obscure to the Roman authorities?

Let us look at and read about Jesus' sayings from this new, postcolonial perspective assuming that Jesus opposed the political/economic world of Rome but often used coded, hidden sayings that only Jews could decipher to challenge the Roman world. We will begin with the blessings of the people and behavior that was exactly the opposite of who and what were prized in the world of Rome.

Jesus sought to unite his peasant audience with wisdom for daily living and survival, including sayings such as our propensity to seek the speck in our neighbor's eye while we have a beam in our own. Walls' *The Glass Castle* is a helpful example of applying Jesus' wisdom against blaming parents and others rather than accepting responsibility for our actions and getting on with our lives.

3. See Crossan, *The Greatest Prayer*.

4. Scott, *Dominations*, 184.

5. Ibid.

6. Horsley, *Jesus in Context*, 125.

Part One

Jesus' Wisdom on Blessings

3

Introduction

PART ONE WILL FOCUS on the Beatitudes in the gospels of Matthew and Luke. First, I present a preview of those blessings in the wisdom of Mary, which is found only in Luke. It is called the Magnificat or Mary's song. Although the Magnificat is not specifically the wisdom of Jesus, it is, like the Beatitudes, what Luke remembered and reported decades after Jesus' death, and it gives us a good introduction to Jesus' mission and to wisdom in the spirit of Jesus. I have sculpted the Magnificat and Beatitudes in modern costume (except for the sculpture of Mary and Elizabeth who are in period costumes) so they may translate more directly to our time. However, I will continue to stress the political/economic context of Jesus' time and our time, their differences and similarities.

Another reminder of those differences between the first century and our western, twenty-first century shows us that then:

1. Empires were dominated by brute force, violence and fear.
2. Slavery was legal.
3. There was no middle class.
4. Patriarchy ruled.
5. There was no separation of religion and the state.
6. People identified themselves by groups (family, tribe, religion, ethnicity), not as individuals as we do.

Yet there are similarities between the first century and our time. Now:

1. Empires still rule by force and even more by economic domination. Such rule is now euphemistically called a country's "sphere of influence."
2. War is still perpetual.

3. Corruption still reigns in governments and mega-corporations that are "too big to fail."
4. Might still is deemed right in international relations.
5. Religion is separate from the state but is still used to justify political/economic systems.

With these essentials in mind, the Magnificat and the Beatitudes can be seen as revolutionary. I begin with the Magnificat.

4

The Magnificat

Introduction

EIGHT OF MY SCULPTURES of the Magnificat are now on the wall of Seminary Hall at Drew Theological School in Madison, New Jersey.

How do we "say" the unspeakable magnificence of God's blessings or "speak" of the most radiant events in our lives? According to the Gospel of Luke, Mary had such a glorious experience when she learned of the coming birth of her child, Jesus. Of course, it is not likely that the writer of this Magnificat was present to hear the exact words of an unknown peasant girl when he sat down to write them some eighty-five years later. But Luke had a model for Mary's Song in the Song of Hannah when she gave birth to Samuel and offered him to God (1 Sam 2:1–10). The many similarities between the two show that Luke used some of Hannah's words for Mary's song. Both exult, rejoice, and praise God in the highest way. Both call for lifting up the feeble, the poor, the needy, and lowly. Both call for bringing down the arrogant, the proud, and the mighty.

Hannah and Mary are presented in the Bible speaking the magnificence of God's blessings in the ancient words that are a miraculous gift to us. They are words of pure gladness. ("My soul magnifies the Lord, and my spirit rejoices in God my Savior," Luke 1:46.) They are so joyous that they merit repeating in more ways than in words, in the arts of all kinds. In these sculptures I seek to do that, recognizing that our theological culture is very word oriented.

The survival of these words in the Magnificat is indeed a miraculous gift because, in addition to their overwhelming happiness, they are also bluntly revolutionary and political. The proud are scattered, the powerful are brought down from their thrones, the rich are sent away empty. The poor and lowly take their place. That kind of revolution is one that the mighty kings and emperors who sponsored Bible translations would wisely have left out. But the words have survived and now challenge us today to make the most of them. I have sought to do so in today's images and today's world of violence and corruption, which is to be overthrown by the gladness and glory of God's blessings to us.

Mary and Elizabeth

Mary visits her cousin Elizabeth, both pregnant. Elizabeth dances with John, and Mary, pregnant with Jesus, sings the Magnificat (Luke 1:46–55).

Spirit Rejoice

According to scholars Mary was probably quite young, maybe only fourteen, when she became pregnant. So I do not imagine her sitting demurely reading a book as in many annunciation paintings. A young girl might more likely rejoice by dancing or turning a cartwheel. My sculpture of her shows such an exuberant girl full of joy at this news of God's blessing her with Jesus' birth and her special election as his mother. She is mid air with her hair and scarf flying loose. We, like Mary, can feel the great joy in learning of One coming who will bring the peace, justice, and wholeness for which we all yearn. He will do this by the example of his words, deeds, and his very life. This great news calls for jumping for joy.

Favor the Lowly

Great news for the lowly. But by all our usual standards, the rich and famous are favored and privileged, not the lowly or servants of other people. This was also the case in the Roman Empire. Anyone who claimed that a peasant girl of a conquered nation was favored or privileged would be considered to be joking or delusional. I see that peasant girl as quite lowly, by normal standards, scrubbing a bathroom floor on her knees, but looking up in hope toward a small, barred window. Mary considers herself blessed and the receiver of great things from God—the reward for those who fear God rather than honoring the Empire.

Scatter the Proud

Those who rule by violence and fear proudly bully the weak and poor and are eager to show off their strength. But Mary claims the opposite. It is God who has the strength and it is this Holy One who scatters the proud bullies of the world. In my sculpture, one such bullying ruler proudly basks in his natty suit but is really so insecure that a heavily armed squad of soldiers must protect him.

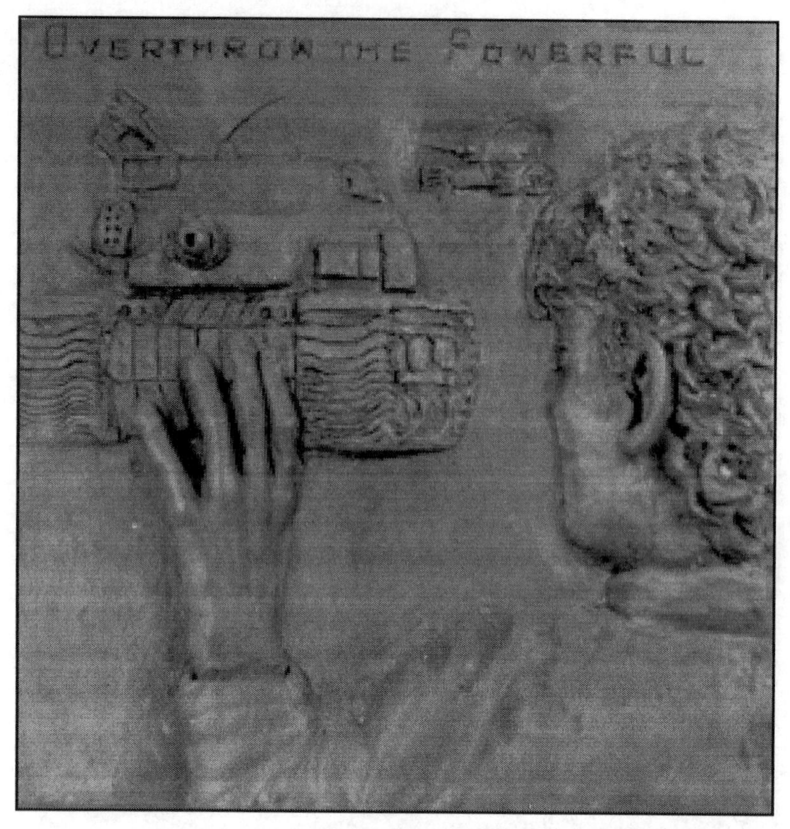

Overthrow Powerful

Perhaps this radical passage survived the centuries because the powerful paid little attention to a girl's voice. But the power of nonviolent resistance has worked to overthrow the powerful in recent times in India, the Philippines, Eastern Europe, Egypt, and Tunisia. This image of an unarmed person stopping heavily armed tanks is one modern image of such a nonviolent force and reminds us, for example, of courageous individuals at Tiananmen Square. The viewer sees the same violent force in the image of the person in the sculpture. It challenges us to find the courage to resist even the most powerful forces just as Jesus resisted the only superpower of his day, Rome.

Lift the Lowly

The lowly handmaid has stopped scrubbing the bathroom floor, the barred window is open; she now has toilet paper. She has overcome her shame and is joyously sipping a beverage in the tub celebrating the victory of the coming of peace, justice, and wholeness, the long awaited *shalom* of the conquered people. The son of David is coming and the humiliation of her dominated people will end.

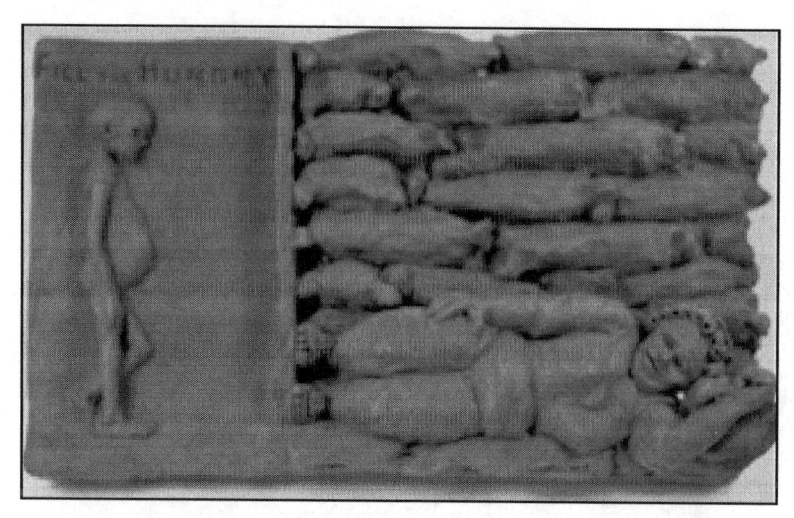

Feed the Hungry

The coming of the anointed one is not only a spiritual gift of words and wishes. It also means that the hungry will have enough to eat. This image contrasts an obese person lying amid sacks of grain with a starving child walking amid nothing. This is happening now because the greedy few horde their wealth and power. But that will end and food will not be used as a weapon or sold only for profit. Rather, hunger will be abolished because food will become a right for all people.

Rich Away Empty

A pastor sends the rich away from this world in a hearse with its door wide open to negative space, suggesting another world. A wind from it blows her hair, but she firmly and grimly carries out her pastoral duty of burying the dead. The rich call such attacks "class warfare," but Jesus makes no such excuses. The rich make the cut about as often as a camel squeezes through the eye of a needle.

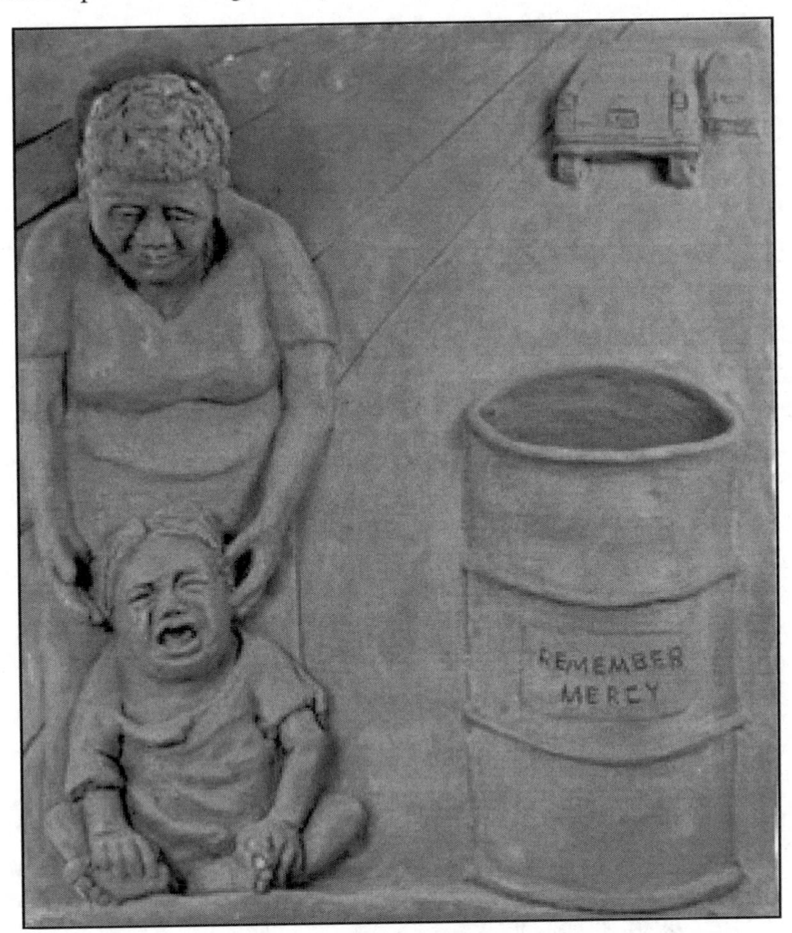

Remember Mercy

Mary's song mentions mercy twice. God is merciful to those who show fear or respect for God, who is merciful to Israel. The meaning for us is translated in the Beatitudes in which the merciful receive mercy. This image shows one act of mercy in which a woman stops her car on a highway to help a helpless baby who has been abandoned, left for trash. We can expect God's mercy when we show others mercy.

5

Introduction to Jesus' Wisdom in the Beatitudes

(Matt 5:1–12; Luke 6:20–26; Gos. Thom. 54, 68, 69)

The Beatitudes in general confirm just how radical Jesus was. Then and now, they confront all conventional wisdom with absolute opposition. We all know, don't we, that poverty is miserable, hunger is awful, grief and crying are very sad, and hatred and persecution are terrible. But Jesus says these are blessings, and that God favors those who suffer these afflictions. Matthew (alone) adds four more virtues that are rewarded but that society rarely values with any privileges. These are meekness, mercy, peacemaking, and purity of heart, virtues he may have gotten from Psalms 24:3–6 and 37:11.

The first four (or five depending on whether one counts hatred and persecution separately) Beatitudes are probably from the Q sayings. Both Matthew and Luke have them. They are: the poor, hungry, mourners, and the persecuted/hated. But these two gospels differ in their location of Jesus' preaching of them: on the Mountain (Matthew) or the plain (Luke); and Luke uses the second person, "you" (as in "blessed are you who are poor"), while Matthew uses the third person, "the poor" or "those" (as in "blessed are the poor in spirit" with one exception in the Beatitude on Persecution). Matthew adds "in spirit." Thomas has three Beatitudes, addressed to the poor, the hungry, and the persecuted, though they are not grouped together as in Matthew and Luke.

The four that Matthew added are virtues that will be rewarded (e.g. the merciful receive mercy) as distinct from the first five, which are afflictions that will be relieved (e.g. hunger will be satisfied). The Beatitudes are doublets in that each one names who or what is blessed on the one hand, and, on the other, the reason for the blessing. This doublet form suggests a visual representation of two-sided relief sculptures. So I made nine double pieces with eighteen images, front and back.

6

Jesus' Wisdom on the Poor

"Blessed are you who are poor,
for yours is the kingdom of God."

(Luke 6:20b; also Gos. Thom. 54; Matt 5:3)

As a privileged person I have not experienced real poverty or destitution. I have had to scrimp and work hard most of the time, but I now own a nice home and always have plenty to eat. I learned what poverty was really like on the Lakota reservation where I go often to learn and teach native pastors and pastors-to-be. When I was starting these trips, one of the pastors of three small churches drove four hours from Eagle Butte to Rapid City, SD to pick us up in his old Ford van. The topic for this session was Postcolonial Theology. I learned from this native pastor, who was in his late 70s, that he was still parenting two of his grandchildren. When he was not caring for them, he was driving all over the reservation dealing with one crisis after another, including suicides, car wrecks, and even murder. As we concluded the seminar with a communion service together, he in Lakota, I in English, I began to think of him as a saint. If only we Protestants had saints! I was convinced of his sainthood when he drove us back to the airport in Rapid City and shared more of his life.

But before we hear his story, let us look more closely at the Beatitude on the poor and the issue of poverty in the U.S. The United States is deeply divided over the issue of the poor. Why? Because the division is a deeply moral one between the so-called political left and right. The clearest statement defining this division I have found is by Paul Krugman, Nobel laureate in economics, Princeton University professor, and columnist for the *New York Times*. He writes,

> One side of America politics considers the modern welfare state . . . morally superior to the capitalism . . . we had before the New Deal. It's only right . . . for the affluent to help the less fortunate.
>
> The other side believes that people have a right to keep what they earn, and taxing them to support others, no matter how needy, amounts to theft. . . . many activists on the right really do see taxes and regulation as tyrannical impositions on their liberty.[1]

This is not to say that the "right" has no concern for the poor, (some do, some don't), but those on the "right" usually see charity as a personal matter for individuals to decide, not a public issue for the government to tax and regulate. Krugman is clearly on the side of the "left" as am I. But what do you readers think is the best way to deal with poverty? And what does the Bible, and especially Jesus' wisdom, say about how we are to treat the poor? Is it by private charity or by government taxation and regulation? Or is there a middle ground between these polar opposite moral positions?

Fig 11: Blessed are you who are poor,

yours is the Kingdom of God.

The Bible can be and most often is read as private, spiritual wisdom that has little or nothing to do with public, governmental matters. Indeed, Matthew's version of the first Beatitude is: "Blessed are the

1. Krugman, "A Tale of Two Moralities."

poor *in spirit*." That seems to limit our concern to spiritual rather than physical or material matters of poverty. There are three responses to this perspective:

First, the Bible does not separate the spiritual and material. To be poor is dispiriting then and now. Matthew did not ignore material poverty in favor of spiritual poverty, for he reports Jesus' frequent efforts to feed people (Matt 12:1–8; 14:13–21; 15:32–39; 26:20–29). Second, neither Luke nor Thomas adds "in spirit," which leaves us a choice of whom to follow. Which gospel is closer to Jesus' wisdom? Probably Luke and Thomas. Third, New Testament scholar, John Dominic Crossan believes that Matthew added "in spirit" to Jesus' saying, but Crossan goes on to make another point: "The basic problem is not just Matthew's gloss [addition] "in spirit," although that certainly diverts attention and interpretation from material to spiritual, from economic to religious poverty. Even when that is left aside as a Matthean addition, there is still a serious problem with the word *poor* itself."[2]

Crossan gives a helpful and detailed analysis of the Greek words for the poor (*ptōchos* or *penēs*). The essence of his analysis is that the word for "poor" in the Beatitudes would be translated more accurately as "disparate, unclean, degraded and expendable." So it is not just the people who are poor but still managing to cope with basic needs (*penēs*) but the really destitute that Jesus says are blessed. Crossan sees this softening of (*ptōchos*) to being poor but coping, rather than destitute, as a way to spiritualize poverty. I think it is a grave error to spiritualize poverty. To do so is simply an excuse of the affluent to ignore poverty and think that Jesus did too. When Jesus says the destitute are God's favorite, it means that we are to get serious about treating God's favorites with the dignity, respect, and aid that helps them get out of poverty.

When the native pastor drove us in his rumbling old van back to the airport, he recited more of his life journey, but he seemed especially happy that day and explained why. He said he had just gotten a new home. He was finally able to move into a trailer home with his wife, granddaughters, and two other children. A trailer home was a great improvement on his former living space. For me, that hit home. I was shocked because I live in a comfortable house instead of a trailer. I think Jesus' message in this Beatitude is "Whatever it takes, private charity and public, government taxes and regulations, make sure all people, espe-

2. Crossan, *The Historical Jesus*, 270.

cially native people whose land our government took from them, have a decent home in which to live." Private charity is commendable but arbitrary. If the government can *take* native land from them, it must also *give back* at least enough aid to end such poverty.

This image is a two-sided relief sculpture of a beggar. Rather than his head, it is his hand reaching for aid that is circled with a halo, symbolizing our sacred obligation to meet the needs of the poor. When he learns of his blessedness, when he learns that God does not shame him but favors him, he dances in the hope that we will end his poverty, for he is one of God's favorites.

7

Jesus' Wisdom on Hunger

"Blessed are you who are hungry now,
for you will be filled."
(Luke 6:21a; also Matt 5:6; Gos. Thom. 69)

I HAVE BEEN MODERNIZING and personalizing the wisdom sayings of Jesus, but I am especially challenged to do so with the blessing on hunger. For I and most people I know have always had enough to eat except perhaps for a few times when we have chosen to fast. Once I fasted for two days as part of a peace demonstration. (Since I was in a leadership role, I needed to do my part and participate fully.) I remember having started without breakfast the first day and developing a headache before noon, then a stomach ache before dark, followed by dizziness the first evening. What was most unpleasant to me was that I could not think straight for lack of food. Very little entered my head except images of food. I could barely imagine how so many people in the world endure these hunger pangs all of the time when I thought that I might not be able to hold to the fast a second day.

It is important to compare Luke and Matthew's versions of this Beatitude, for Matthew, who added "in spirit" to the Beatitude on the poor, here adds, "and thirst for righteousness" to "blessed are those who hunger" (5:6). This appears to spiritualize this Beatitude, making it seem to be about a spiritual attitude rather than about physical hunger and food to fill empty stomachs. However, to "hunger and thirst for righteousness" or justice also means to feed the hungry who are among "the least of these" (Matt 25:35–45). Matthew appears only to spiritualize this Beatitude for he reports that Jesus gave out food abundantly, not based on social standing but based on need. He especially gave food to the lowly and the outcasts with whom he frequently ate meals. The Gospel of John reports that some of the last words of the resurrected Jesus were about food. He tells Peter three times to feed or tend his sheep (21:15–17). Jesus' followers likewise are to show their love for him by feeding those who are hungry, in so doing making God's Beatitude real.

Fig. 12: Blessed are the hungry.

You will be filled.

We have been studying the wisdom of Jesus through a dual lens of economics and politics. Hunger, food production, and access to food are economic and political matters that affect us both privately and publicly. Who controls access to food is a life and death issue. As with the Beatitude on the poor, the hungry are to be blessed in God's Empire where they will be filled.

Josephus, from whom we learn the history of first-century Jewish people, was himself a Jew but is considered to be sympathetic to Rome. However, he was critical of some emperors such as Gaius Caligula (who died 41 C.E.) and records an event during Gaius' reign as emperor that illustrates the domination of Rome and its limits when it is confronted with nonviolent tactics that are firmly employed. Josephus' account also illustrates how Rome was dependent on food production in its colonies, including Judea, and why Jesus' Beatitude on hunger gave hope to those who had little to eat. "Now Caius[1] Caesar did so grossly abuse the fortune he had arrived at, as to take himself to be a god. . . . he sent Petronius with an army to Jerusalem, to place his statues [as Zeus/Jupiter] in the temple and commanded him that, in case the Jews would not admit of them, he should slay those that opposed it, and carry all the rest of the nation into captivity."[2]

Petronius was the Legate of Syria and he obediently left Antioch with "three legions and many Syrian auxiliaries"[3] and headed to Jerusalem to place the statue of Gaius in the temple. However, the Jews opposed this as the greatest of sacrileges. They told Petronius that they were prepared to die rather than accept it. Then they went on strike and refused to plant their crops. Their strike went on for weeks all the while with Petronius and his 18,000-plus army poised to attack the striking peasants.

Roman ideology claimed to provide food for all, but in reality theirs was a top-down hierarchical system that rewarded the rich and left the poor to fend for themselves. There were exceptions that proved this rule as with occasional elite-sponsored food handouts whose primary purpose was to elevate the social standing of the benefactor. The prized meat from sacrificed animals was given out according to one's social standing; the rich got the best cuts, the poor what was left. Even the location of one's seat at civic meals was determined by one's economic and political position. Jesus specifically attacked this practice (Luke 14:7–11). Warren Carter elaborates on the political use of food in Jesus' time.

> Quality and plentiful food was a marker of status and wealth . . . that divided elites from nonelites. It established the former as privileged and powerful and the latter as inferior and of low entitlement. The latter struggled to acquire enough food as well as food of adequate nutritional value. For most, this was a constant struggle. And it was cyclic whereby most dropped below subsistence levels at times throughout the year. Food, then, displayed the injustice of the empire on a daily basis. The irony of this situation was that Roman propaganda claimed that one of

1. Whether to spell Caligula's other name with a "C" or a "G" is unsettled.
2. Josephus, *War*, 2.185.
3. Ibid., 2.186.

> the gifts of the Roman Empire to its inhabitants was fertility and abundance![4]

After many weeks during the planting season when they refused to plant their crops, the Jewish peasants convinced Petronius to defy Caesar and thereby risk his own life and call off the plan to install Caesar's statue in the temple. He would likely be killed for disobeying Caesar. In addition, the crops had to be planted or else all would suffer for lack of food. As Josephus put it, Petronius

> saw that the country was in danger of lying without tillage (for it was about seed-time that the multitude continued for fifty days together idle,) so he at last got them together, and told them, that it was best for him to run some hazard himself: "for either, by the divine assistance, I shall prevail with Caesar, and shall myself escape the danger as well as you . . . or, in case Caesar continues his rage, I will be ready to expose my own life for such a great number as you are."[5]

The nonviolent resistance worked. Petronius withdrew his troops to Antioch and sent a letter telling Caesar that the plan was interrupted. In addition, Petronius' life was spared because Gaius Caligula was assassinated before the letter reached him. The peasants returned to plant their crops and feed the people with what food was left after they paid taxes, tributes, rents, and tithes that were usually paid in kind. This Beatitude tells us that, by contrast, when God's Empire comes, all will feast at God's banquet.

Back to my fast. I was able to stay with it the second day despite my headache, stomach ache, and dizziness. The fast finally ended that evening with a meal of sorts: rice. That was all—no butter, gravy, meat, or vegetables, only rice and some salt. I have never enjoyed anything more than the pile of rice that I devoured. With a little salt, it tasted like a gourmet feast. I began to understand what hunger is like and how, as the Gospel of Thomas puts it, "the stomach of the one in want may be filled" (54:69).

4. Carter, *The Roman Empire and the New Testament*, 110.
5. Josephus, *War* 2.200–1.

8

Jesus' Wisdom on Mourning

"Blessed are those who mourn, for they will be comforted."

(Matt 5:4; also Luke 6:21b)

MY FRIEND AND I went to school together and shared many things over many years. Now he was dying of leukemia in a Baltimore hospital. His spouse was at his side for days watching him become weaker and weaker. The doctors were keeping him alive with tubes going into his body. It was so sad and painful to see this vital and highly intelligent friend confined to his bed with no hope for recovery. I understood but was still amazed at what his spouse did for her last goodbye to him and how she survived the loss of her husband and a number of other losses that would have destroyed many other people.

But first a look at the text of this Beatitude.

This saying about how those who mourn will be comforted is, no doubt, from the sayings in Q. Scholars think that Luke's version of "Blessed are those who cry, for you will laugh" may be closer to Jesus,[1] and Crossan translates the saying with "sad" and "weep" rather than "mourn," as in Matthew in the NRSV, and concludes that this saying is "almost synonymous" with the Beatitudes on hunger and poverty.[2] Yet he believes all three are directly from Jesus.

Mourning is all about loss that brings sadness, weeping, and crying; and the greatest loss is, of course, the death of a loved one. How can such loss be comforted and how can crying become laughter? I think the

1. Patterson, *The God of Jesus*, 96.

2. Crossan, *The Historical Jesus*, 273.

answer lies in another saying of Jesus: "Do not store up for yourselves treasures on earth . . ." (Matt 6:19). My friend's spouse said this passage helped her get through her loss. In order to lose something and thus mourn its loss with sadness and crying and a lack of comfort, one must hold that treasure or loved one as essential to one's own identity and being. If a person believes that she cannot live without that treasure or person, she loses some or all of her self or soul when she loses that treasure or person. Thus, one believes that the treasure or loved one has become central to one's existence. That includes one's self-orientation, and one's life compass. Such a loss cannot be replaced or repaired, but it can be let go so that one can find the comfort of this Beatitude.

In order to lose something we must first have it. To be sure, there is nothing wrong with having things. It is only when those things *have us* that our mourning cannot be comforted. When we turn our souls over to things and to other people, there is no consolation when one's soul is lost. So the saying about not storing up treasures on earth makes sense. If we do not hold any thing or any person as absolutely essential to our own existence, then our mourning is consolable. We can have a life after we let go of what (or whomever) we have lost. So we do well not to hold anything on earth so tightly that we are destroyed by the loss of it.

If that is so, then what, if anything, can we count on absolutely? To what can we cling and in what can we believe in such a way that we are not destroyed by its loss? To what can we give ourselves that does not die? Clearly the answer is eternal things that are not limited by time or space. Love is one such eternal thing. And the love we have shared with a loved one need not die with that person's visible demise. To the extent that we cling to such eternal things we can be consoled. We "will be comforted." We can be reborn to a new life after a loss. This we can see in friends who have overcome great loss, as I observed in the spouse of my friend.

Such renewal or rebirth is not only a private, personal matter but public and social as well. We grow up and find our identity in the values of national, racial, class, and ethnic groups that nurture us. Some people hold these invisible values and worldviews so deeply that they will sometimes kill and die for them. However, they are not eternal values. Again and again the Bible reminds us that nations, principalities, powers, kings, and princes, and even the chosen people of Israel, all fall and die. What is eternal is only God (and God's attributes, such as love).

My friend died around the time I was working on these sculptures of the Beatitudes. I mourned his loss very much as he was my best friend and my son's Godfather. But I found some comfort in my opportunity to sculpt a piece on the Beatitude "Blessed are those who mourn." I was guided by the image of my friend's spouse and her last good bye. She asked the doctors to remove the tubes they had placed in and around his head and began to stroke his face. It was the saddest image I had ever known, yet it was also the most tender and most loving gesture possible.

Fig.13: Blessed are the Mourners.

They will be comforted.

I made the sculpture of this Beatitude with this image seared in my mind. In this two-sided relief sculpture, my friend is still present and real though his image is in negative space symbolizing the spiritual realm where he lives eternally. His spouse's hands embrace him. On the reverse side, the larger hands of God in turn comfort her. I think she was comforted as the Beatitude promises, for she has, since her husband's death, displayed what I judge to be a miraculous strength by moving on to an active, committed life she shares with their daughters and grandchildren, and in community activities. What continues to amaze me is how she has also overcome additional devastating losses. She not only lost her husband but also both of her parents. In addition, her house burned down along with all her possessions—all within a period of four years. Where has she found the strength to handle all this? She told me that she often recited the wisdom mentioned above: "Do not store up for yourselves treasures on earth. . . ." Just as I modeled this sculpture after the image of her last goodbye, I hope to model my life and spirit after her powerful resilience when losses come my way. She also told me that, like her husband, a Hebrew Bible scholar, she drew strength from a passage in Jeremiah: "Their life shall become like a watered garden, and they shall never languish again" (31:12b). Both were avid gardeners, and that made the passage a mantra for him through his suffering and for her after her loss.

When she and her daughter asked me, I was honored to make another version of this sculpture for them and later to baptize her granddaughter in my friend's stead. At that service I was absorbed in his spirit because I was in his place and it seemed that I was expected to represent him. At that baptism his spirit was very much present, and we all were comforted by it. Our mourning had been replaced with comfort, even laughter. But most of all, his spouse's miraculous recovery has to inspire anyone who has eyes to see.

9

Jesus' Wisdom on Persecution and Hatred

"Blessed are those who are persecuted."

(Matt 5:10)

"Blessed are those who are persecuted for righteousness sake,
for theirs is the Kingdom of heaven. Blessed are you when
people revile you and persecute you and utter all kinds of
evil against you falsely on my account. Rejoice and be glad,
for your reward is great in heaven, for in the same way they
persecuted the prophets who were before you."

(Also, Luke 6:22–23; Gos. Thom. 68:1–2; 69:1)

In Kathryn Stockett's bestselling book, *The Help*, Aibileen is an African American maid or "help" working for a white family in Jackson, Mississippi in the 1960s. The author reports Aibileen, Minny, and other maids' side of the story and what it feels like to endure persecution—the daily hatred, reviling, exclusion, and defamation by white people in a system of segregation and white supremacy. The book shows how all-encompassing the white supremacy system is. It includes below minimum wages for the "help," threats of attack, real attacks, imprisonment, and small, degrading insults in daily communication. Terror, fear, humiliation, and suppressed anger rule their daily lives.

Aibileen's boss, Miss Leefolt has a new bathroom added for Aibileen to use for fear that the family might catch some disease from her in the family bathroom. When the time comes to tell Aibileen that she must henceforth use only this new bathroom, Miss Leefolt frames it as a special favor, as something for Aibileen's benefit. Now she can have her very own bathroom, a tiny plywood box outside in the car port. The black maids in their white uniforms cannot complain for fear that their white bosses will use their "tool kit" of persecution. Unlike white male physical violence and terror such as the cold-blooded murder of Medgar Evers in his Jackson, Mississippi front yard in 1963, the white women's "tool kit" of persecution keeps them from getting their hands dirty with physical violence, but it is violent persecution nonetheless.

The two Beatitudes on persecution and hatred are mixed together in Matthew and Thomas. Luke includes hatred, exclusion, reviling, and defamation, but not persecution. Luke does not mention persecution here, perhaps to keep favor with Rome, as he does elsewhere in Luke/Acts. The usual interpretation of Luke's list of mistreatments can be and often is privatized. Matthew and Thomas can be and often are spiritualized to read as persecution that is for "righteousness' sake" and persecution that is "in their hearts," respectively. However, there was no separation between private and public, spiritual and material in biblical times. "Righteousness" included public good and is better translated as "justice," which has a more public connotation in our time. Thomas' "persecutions in our hearts" suggests what we now call "internalization" of that persecution. That is, those who are persecuted come to believe they deserve it. They blame themselves for their mistreatment. The main point of these Beatitudes is that according to Jesus and the prophets those who are persecuted, hated, excluded, reviled, and defamed in the imperial world are blessed and honored in God's world.

How can this be? How can the persecuted be blessed? Who would want to be persecuted? When people suffer persecution, they can give in to it, internalize and submit to it, or they can resist the persecution. When resistance multiplies and collects into a critical mass, it is a powerful force. Jesus taught such resistance but it was always nonviolent resistance. To believe in righteousness/justice is to anticipate that God's Empire of justice will come. As Martin Luther King, Jr. says the arc of moral history bends toward justice. The proof of this is the extremes to which imperial powers go to assure that the people do submit and internalize, spiritualize, and privatize persecution. Religion is often recruited to justify this privatization and spiritualization of persecution.

I made two two-sided sculpture reliefs of this Beatitude. The first one focuses on the list in Luke of hatred, exclusion, reviling, and defamation.

Fig 14: Blessed are you when people hate you. . . .

Leap for joy.

On this first side a domineering man verbally attacks a girl. She huddles in fear and shame, internalizing the abuse. On the second side she has dismissed the persecution and, as Luke says, she rejoices and leaps for joy. It is easy to see how these Beatitudes can be limited to private, individual mistreatment; of course, persecution is personal. But it is *also public* persecution of whole groups of people.

For the second sculpture I thought very long about which group of people to represent as persecuted. There are so many. I finally concluded that the persecution of children is high on the list as they are so vulnerable. I chose an especially awful way children are persecuted. They are made into child soldiers. This is done all over the world, but is most prevalent in Africa, where 10 to 14-year-old boys are given drugs and guns and made to kill. On the first side of this sculpture, such a boy with a gun represents all child soldiers. This one is most unhappy about his fate. On the second side he is quite happy and blessed because he has been freed from being made a soldier. His gun has been absorbed into the jungle vines, and he celebrates his freedom, for his reward is great in God's Empire.

Fig. 15: Blessed are those who are persecuted. . .

theirs is the Kingdom of Heaven.

The other group of persecuted people much closer to home in the USA is African American women who "help" white families do housekeeping jobs that whites do not want to do. If the "help" complains, they run great risks of persecution. In the aforementioned story, *The Help*, when the maids do cross a line, the white women bosses of the black maids take their time in conveying that, unlike white men who tend immediately to attack. Aibileen sums up their persecution:

> "First thing a white lady gone do is fire you. You upset, but you figure you'll find another job, when things settle down, when the white lady get around to forgetting. You got a month a rent saved. People bring you squash casseroles.
>
> But then a week after you lost your job, you get this little yellow envelope stuck in your screen door. Paper inside say NOTICE OF EVICTION. Ever landlord in Jackson be white and ever one got a white wife that's friends with somebody. You start to panic some then. You still ain't got no job prospects. Everwhere you try, the door slams in your face. And now you ain't got a place to live.
>
> Then it starts to come a little faster.
>
> If you got a note on your car, they gone repossess it.
>
> If you got a parking ticket you ain't paid, you going to jail.
>
> If you got a daughter, maybe you go live with her. She tend to a white family a her own. But a few days later she come home, say, 'Mama? I just got fired.' She look hurt, scared. She don't understand why. You got to tell her it's cause a you.

> Least her husband still working. Least they can feed the baby.
>
> Then they fire her husband. Just another little sharp tool, shiny and fine . . . Weeks pass and nothing, no jobs, no money, no house. You hope this is the end of it, that she done enough, she ready to forget.
>
> It'll be a knock on the door, late at night. It won't be the white lady at the door. She don't do that kind of a thing herself. But while the nightmare's happening . . . you realize something you known all your life: the white lady don't *ever* forget.
>
> And she ain't gone stop till you dead."[1]

Yet, we are all blessed that Martin Luther King, Jr. rose up at this time to lead thousands of us with nonviolent resistance that began to change this persecution. It was only a beginning, of course, but there are no better examples of how Jesus' nonviolent resistance works or how persecution can be resisted and become a blessing.

1. *The Help*, Kathryn Stockett, 161–61.

10

Jesus' Wisdom on Self-Regard and Land

"Blessed are the meek, for they will inherit the earth."

(Matt 5:5; also Ps 37:11)

It is hard to overemphasize how important land was in Jesus' time, for land meant both survival for the many poor, and riches for the wealthy few. His was an agrarian society; land provided food to sustain life, and land was the main source of wealth. Little else could be used to gain income. Jews considered the lands of ancient Palestine as God's gift to them to be tilled and kept by them forever. It was quite literally holy land, a sacred gift.

Scholars agree that Jesus or Matthew probably got this Beatitude from Psalm 37:11 which says, "But the meek shall inherit the land, and delight themselves in abundant prosperity." Otherwise, it is a Beatitude unique to Matthew's gospel.

The word "meek" has been weakened over the centuries to mean passivity and helplessness. However, some scholars translate the original Greek, *πραε's* as "gentle," not meek. In our time one who is a "gentleman" is not considered passive or helpless, but gentle, respectful, and capable.

If we ask, "Gentleness, *as opposed to what?*", we get helpful insights into this Beatitude. It makes sense to oppose the gentleness of Jesus' self-regard over against the self-regard of aristocratic landowners and the Caesars who regarded themselves as gods or agents of god, Jupiter/ Jove. Augustus was named *pontifex maximus* (highest priest) and *pater patriae* (Father of the Fatherland), " 'Son of God', 'God', 'God from God', 'Lord', 'Redeemer', 'Liberator', and 'Savior of the World' . . ."[1] When

1. Crossan, *God and Empire*, 28.

Christians took over the language of the Roman Empire, "they were taking the identity of the Roman emperor and giving it to a Jewish peasant. Either that was a peculiar joke and a very low lampoon, or it was what the Romans called *majestas* and we call high treason."[2]

Paul Zanker, a famous German archeologist, describes the proud and glorious self-regard of Augustus as a priest: "His piety was put on display for every Roman to see. . . . It is astonishing how many portraits of Augustus made during his lifetime, both on coins and as honorific statues, show him veiled in a toga . . . The humble image of Augustus . . . , however, does nothing to conceal the notion that he enjoyed divine powers."[3] This display of Augustus' images was only about his piety. Many other images glorified his accomplishments, especially the military ones. Zanker quotes Appian's description of his parousia, or entry: "Of the honors voted him he accepted an *ovatio* (a solemn procession into the city, or so-called lesser triumph), an annual victory celebration, and a gilded statue. He would be represented in those garments which he had worn at his entry into the city, and the statue would stand atop a column decorated with the beaks of vanquished ships. But the inscription would say that he has restored the peace on land and sea which had for so long been rent with discord."[4]

Compare this divine self-glorification of Caesar's entry to Jesus' self-regard as he made his entry into the city "humble, and mounted on an donkey" (Matt 21:5). Matthew quotes Jesus saying, "Take my yoke upon you, and learn from me; for I am gentle and humble in heart, and you will find rest for your souls" (11:29). Jesus said many times that the "last will be first," in God's Empire (Mark 10:31; Matt 19:30; Luke 13:30). He rebuked lawyers "who like to walk around in long robes, and to be greeted with respect in the marketplaces, and to have the best seats in the synagogues and places of honor at banquets! They devour widows' houses and for the sake of appearance say long prayers" (Mark 12:38–39). And he put down those who prayed in public to be seen by others, and he elevated the tax collector who prayed with great contrition, unlike the Pharisee who told God how good he himself was compared to the tax collector (Luke 18:9–14). Also, compare the gigantic mausoleum of Augustus and the Ara Pacis Augustus (the altar of Augustan peace) in Rome today to the site of Jesus' death on a cross on a waste site. Other emperors were depicted in sculpture as divine beings. For example,

2. Ibid., 28.

3. Zanker, 127–8.

4. Ibid., 41.

Claudius is presented as a god "cosmically controlling Land and Sea."[5] Clearly meekness and gentleness were of higher value to Jesus rather than pompous displays of wealth, rank, and privilege.

The wealthy few were ones who owned vast estates. Since land ownership was the main source of wealth, the rich constantly sought to expand their holdings as citizens by means of foreclosures, and as the empire by means of wars. Thus when in the Beatitudes of Jesus' wisdom the gentle are blessed with inheriting the earth, it is as opposed to the conventional wisdom that asserted that only the proud, wealthy, and aristocratic were blessed with lands and the prosperity from them.

For the sculptural image of this Beatitude, I modeled a peasant plowing a field with oxen, using a primitive wooden plow. In the distant background are soldiers, a jeep, and a watchtower ready to prevent any rebellion and to keep down the downtrodden.

Fig 16: Blessed Are the Gentle.

They Shall Inherit the Land.

On the second side of the sculpture, the peasant has "inherited the earth" and holds up a deed as he gently bows on his knees. A relative runs toward him to celebrate. The oxen rest and the watchtower becomes the deed he has gotten for his efforts at land reform.

In summary, when we seek to understand this Beatitude, it is wise to think of the gentleness of Jesus as opposed to the arrogant self-promotion of Caesar and the wealthy, and also of the critical importance of land for all the people in Jesus' time and our own.

5. Crossan, *In Search of Paul*, 21.

11

Jesus' Wisdom on Mercy

"Blessed are the merciful, for they will receive mercy."

(Matt 5:7)

"Mercy" and "merciful" are very important words in the Bible, occurring about 180 times and used repeatedly in church liturgies in phrases such as "Lord have mercy." This Beatitude is also unique to Matthew, but asking for mercy is a common reason to approach God. We seek mercy to avoid expected punishment of some kind, deserved or not. Mercy is associated with the commuting of a prison sentence as in a reprieve or the staying of an execution. Indeed, in a book on preaching, Randall Nichols defines the word "grace" as an "unexpected reprieve."[1]

That definition gave me an idea for a sculpture. I had a five-foot trunk of an apple tree that I thought I would carve into a young man on death row who had just been granted an unexpected reprieve. Two limbs off the trunk could become his head and right arm. There was just enough wood if I carved the second, left arm behind his back.

1. Nichols, *Building the Word*, 73.

Reprieve

At this same time I was working frantically in the national office of the United Church of Christ in Washington, D.C., my regular, full-time job. And I was living in an apartment at Wesley Seminary, also in Washington, where I was resident artist, part-time. My anxiety increased each day that year because I was soon to "retire" from my regular job. I imagined that when I ended my job I would lose my sense of self, my identity. For even though I had studied the dangers of giving one's whole self to one's job and thought that I would never do such a thing, I was still in panic mode during my last year of regular, full-time work. Soon

I would lose the things that told me who I was, that defined my daily life, and that told me I was ok. I was earning my acceptance as a human being. I was somebody with a title, an office, a desk, and with deadlines and meetings to structure my time, symbols of my self-understanding. Soon I would have no more invitations to speak or to lead retreats, and I would have no clear title to define my role in life except the title I dreaded: "retired." The very word "retired" was for me the same as "retired, old geezer." I had been blessed with these symbols of my employed self for thirty-five years. Now that self-identity, or at least its symbols, was about to end, and I thought that I would disappear. So I did everything I could to deny that retirement was coming soon. I initiated and accepted every speaking engagement I could and spoke on every topic I could think of. I traveled all over the country to make presentations, trying to convince myself that I was not about to disappear, that I still mattered, that I could offer something that people wanted. But without that regular job, where would I be? *Who* would I be? I did not see myself as a driven person with an 800 lb. monkey on his back, but a friend told me just that, and he was right.

Then on the last days before I officially "retired," I moved out of the Wesley apartment, taught a short course at Princeton Center for Continuing Education, put up an exhibit of my sculpture there, began promoting my new book, *Faith Made Visible*, and travelled to Cleveland for my last staff meeting and a big "celebration" of my departure. I returned to New Jersey that evening and flew out of Philadelphia the next day for Hamburg, Germany, where I met my spouse who had gone on ahead of me. In spite of knowing in my head the dangers of too closely identifying with my work, I still believed that having a purpose in life to which you give yourself is one of life's greatest gifts. When I arrived in Germany, I was probably completely exhausted but my fear of "retirement" kept me energized and denying that I was disappearing, that I was no longer a real person. Yet the image of myself as a retired old geezer haunted me as we drove through Germany and Scandinavia.

However, what was really happening to me deep down in my gut ("mercy," *racham,* means "womb" or "compassion" in Hebrew) was a reprieve from this fearful doom of a lost purpose in my life. On the contrary, an enormous gift of grace, a merciful blessing was being handed to me. That gift was a new purpose and new definition of myself as an artist. Of course, I had been merely a "hobby artist," as one curator once called us part-time artists when he rejected my offer to exhibit my work in his gallery. Although I had regularly taken drawing and sculpture classes with models for thirty years and had had my work rigorously critiqued by some very fine art teachers, I had no official degree from an art school, no real gallery contacts, no direct access to the art world. Also, most of the people I knew professionally were part of the Reformed Protestant Church, which had the most iconoclastic tradition. All pictures and sculptures were taken out of Reformed Protestant sanctuaries in the sixteenth and seventeenth centuries, and few have replaced them since.

No matter. My imagined end of life was being reprieved. I was now free to do art full time and claim a rather unique form of art in our time—art that was theologically informed with a focus on social justice. What I had done for decades with words I could now do with images. Rather soon I was spending my whole time drawing, sculpting, and writing on art. This wild, boundless world of visual art opened up and welcomed me to its endless and amazing facets. It was like being reborn to a whole new world. The apple wood sculpture said it all: I was a prisoner on a spiritual death row and had been reprieved.

As we travelled north from Hamburg in Germany to Denmark, Sweden, and Norway, I began really to see and sketch with pen and ink the trees, houses, street scenes, and art in museums all day, every day. In the evenings I got out my small watercolor kit and added the hues I remembered from that day of sketching. We went to every art museum we could find in Scandinavia. I drew hundreds of sketches, filling my sketchbooks. I was in a visual art heaven.

I am sure that I did not earn the mercy of a new purpose that I was given, for we do not *earn* mercy from hard work as we earn a paycheck. It is a gift that I must share any way I can.

When we returned to the U.S., my show was still up at Princeton Seminary, and Professor Nichols saw my wood carving of the death row inmate who had just learned he was reprieved from execution. I told him how his idea of grace as "unexpected reprieve" had inspired this piece. He bought the sculpture immediately.

I did not disappear as I had thought I would. Rather, I was given the mercy of a new life of art. It was truly a gift of grace, an unexpected reprieve. That purpose of expressing in images what I had written and spoken about in words in my first vocation became my new identity. I finally lost my fear of being lost.

On a level below my consciousness and only available to hindsight, I celebrated this reprieve, this merciful blessing, by carving two wooden pieces that I called "Jubilation." One was about three feet high . . .

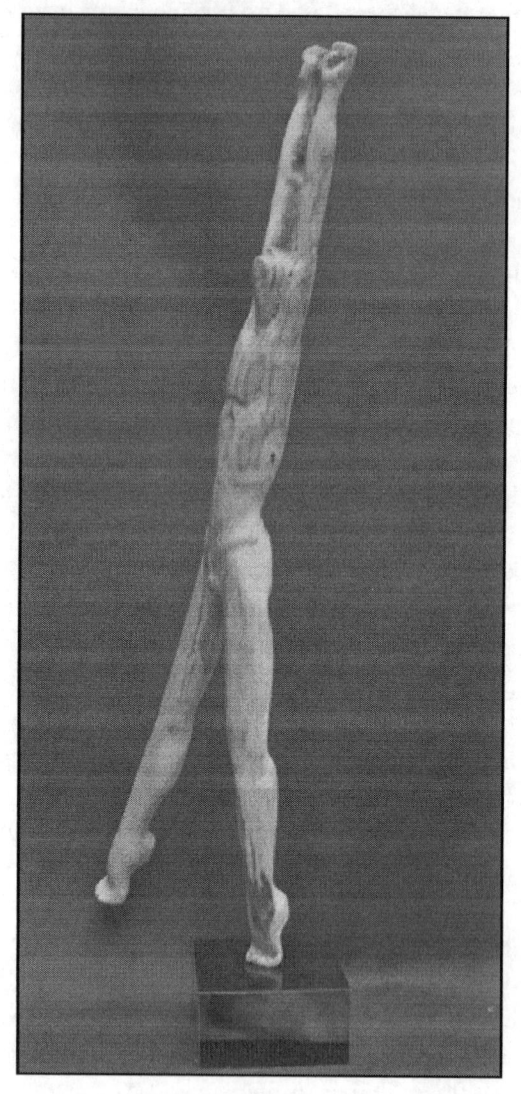

Jubilation.

. . . the other about six. "Jubilation" seemed a fitting name because it means "retirement" in Spanish, but also something to celebrate jubilantly.

Later, when the 9/11 attacks happened, I was resident artist at Andover Newton Theological Seminary and was making the nine, two-sided relief sculptures of the Beatitudes. The more I heard about the amazing sacrifices of the first responders at the Twin Towers, the more I knew I had to sculpt something on the mercy given and received by them, particularly the firemen. I studied hundreds of images and made a composite image on side one of a fireman rescuing a woman as the towers, now in negative space, disappeared. Like all those who mercifully tried to save others, he was totally exhausted. On the second side, another fireman is giving him mercy amid the smoldering ruins of ground zero. Indeed, "Blessed are the merciful for they will receive mercy."

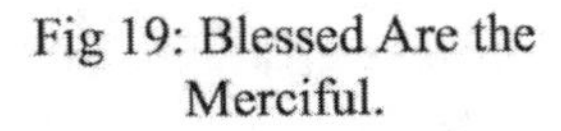

Fig 19: Blessed Are the Merciful.

They Shall Receive Mercy.

12

Jesus' Wisdom on Purity of Heart and How to See God

"Blessed are the pure in heart, for they will see God."

(Matt 5:8)

THIS BEATITUDE IS THE most abstract of them all, and it takes some effort to unpack its meaning. As before, to understand biblical mysteries and abstract sayings, I find it helpful to ask the question, "This . . . as opposed to what?" A pure heart looks like what, as opposed to an impure heart? One of the clearest examples of an impure heart that I have read is found in Josephus' *Antiquities of the Jews* and *The War of the Jews* where he describes King Herod's acts of an impure heart doing pure evil. These passages also illustrate well the wretched political context of Jesus' time, a counterpoint to Jesus' Beatitudes. It is worth an extensive quotation. Herod's violent behavior would be diagnosed in our time as deep paranoia and insane self-defense against all supposed enemies. Josephus reports that Herod forbade

> the citizens either to meet together, or to walk, or eat together, but watched everything they did, and when any were caught, they were severely punished; and many there were who were brought to the citadel Hyrcania, both openly and secretly, and were there put to death; and there were spies set everywhere, both in the city and in the roads, who watched those that met together; nay, it is reported that he did not himself neglect this part of caution, but that he would oftentimes himself take the habit of a private man, and mix among the multitude, in the nighttime, and make trial what opinion they had of his government; and as for those

> that could no way be reduced to acquiesce under his scheme of government, he persecuted them all manner of ways; but for the rest of the multitude, he required that they should be obliged to take an oath of fidelity to him, and at the same time compelled them to swear that they would bear him good will . . . but for such as . . . had indignation at the force he used to them, he by one means or another made away with them. [1]

Then as Herod lay dying he

> proceeded to attempt a horrid wickedness; for he got together the most illustrious men of the whole Jewish nation, out of every village, into a place called Hippodrome, and there shut them in. He then called for his sister Salome . . . [and said] "to send soldiers to encompass these men that are now in custody, and slay them immediately upon my death, and then all Judea, and every family of them, will weep . . ."[2]

Thus the wickedness of Herod's impure heart led him not only to kill potential opponents in his lifetime but to order the continuation of the murder even after his death, for the selfish goal of having a "splendid funeral."[3] Such an impure heart that needs to kill in order that he might have a better funeral helps us see more clearly its opposite in the report of the pure heart of Jesus and other martyrs who do not *take* other lives but *give* their own lives for others' sake. For Jesus' pure heart could see God in all people, even enemies. Herod's heart appears to have been so impure that he had to destroy any suspected opponent. He could not see God in others. Others were only objects to serve his whims. By contrast, Jesus' heart must have been so pure that he had to heal and support all people, especially the oppressed. He could see God in all people. Herod was blind to God in others, whereas Jesus saw God without limits.

Comparing Herod's blindness, murder, and paranoia to Jesus' vision of openness and caring for others helps me make sense of the Beatitude in which a pure heart such as Jesus' sees God. This Beatitude is only in Matthew and some scholars believe he is the author of it rather than Jesus. However, it certainly is true to Jesus' wisdom, and Jesus has always been seen as its originator. The Beatitude also follows prophetic tradition as seen in Jeremiah (31:33) where he calls for the law to be written on our

1. Josephus, *Ant.*, 15.366–68.
2. Josephus, *War*, 1.659–60.
3. Ibid., 1.660.

hearts. And Jesus' own saying: "the good person out of the good treasure of the heart produces good" (Luke 6:45a) makes the same point. In a word, when the basic core of a person or people can see holiness (God) around them and in others, they honor all of life and serve the good of all others rather than defend themselves and attack others.

"Seeing God" in all creation is for me what visual art is about. John Updike, the famous writer, also studied and wrote on art. He said, "What is art supposed to do except make us say, Wow!—to strip the skin of dullness from what we see?"[4] That "skin of dullness" can become a blindness of the soul that cannot see the holy in people or nature. But when art helps us to see the glory of creatures and creation, it is doing what we try to do in preaching: to open ourselves to the vision of God, to see again that Empire of Goodness.

I will illustrate this purity of heart and seeing God with a story. My friend George (Bill) Webber graced my life at the close of his own. I knew him only in his "retirement" years when he was no longer president of New York Seminary or heading the East Harlem Protestant Parish. But I knew about his earlier good works from his books and his general reputation as a saintly man. He volunteered to work on social justice issues with me on the national staff of the United Church of Christ. He and his spouse, Helen, continued to live in East Harlem, where they took me in to their tiny apartment one night.

The next morning as I was brushing my teeth in their small bathroom, I noticed piles of small bottles of shampoo like the ones in hotel rooms. Afterwards I also saw many little bags of peanuts and pencils. Bill always seemed to have his pockets full of these "free" items he collected on his frequent airline travels. I eventually learned that he gathered these small items for the prisoners at Sing Sing Prison. These prisoners were his "flock" who were in an educational program he founded there. He taught courses at Sing Sing for years to enable the prisoners to have a constructive life when they were eventually freed. And he brought these small gifts with him on his visits.

Bill never promoted himself. He never appeared to need to do so; he seemed always to know God affirmed him and that was all that mattered to him—although he had a plenty to brag about. Instead, he relentlessly promoted others. When he filled in for me at a speaking engagement in Iowa once, his report of the event was that the learners there were

4. Updike, "The Artist as Showman," 52.

disappointed at my absence. I knew this to be at least a white lie if not pure hooey. But Bill seemed to live in a different world untouched by the fame, fads, gossip, or celebrities in the current news cycle. Once he unwittingly stood in line at an airport next to a glamorous movie star and enjoyed a pleasant conversation with her. He only discovered who she was later when we told him at a staff meeting.

When I try to illustrate in words the meaning of this Beatitude, "Blessed are the pure in heart," I think of Bill. And I think of Jesus who always lifted others up to support and encourage them, never worrying about himself in this life or the next. They were so centered and self-affirming that they had no need to defend themselves as Herod did and many of the rest of us do.

When I thought of how to illustrate this Beatitude in images, I came up with a girl who is blind and trapped behind bars as one way of showing the blindness of an impure heart. The image on one side of this relief sculpture depicts her surrounded with a nimbus (here shown by the negative space) suggesting the holiness (God within) and a pure heart.

Fig 20: Blessed are the Pure in Heart.

They Shall See God.

On the other side, the girl is out of this prison, her eyes now see and her hands welcome the blessings of the sight of God, Jesus' own vision, in which God is always within sight.

Blessedly, when Herod finally died in 4 CE, his more pure-hearted sister refused to carry out his instructions to murder the Jewish leaders. Instead, she set them free.

13

Jesus' Wisdom on Making Peace

"Blessed are the peacemakers,
for they will be called the children of God."

(Matt 5:9; also Psalm 37:37)

We knelt to pray in the U.S. Capitol Rotunda in Washington, D.C. to protest the war in Nicaragua, one of a long history of U.S. military interventions in Central America in support of corporate interests there. Our protest was against the Contra War that supported the corporation-friendly Somosa dictatorship against the leftist Sandinistas. We knew it was illegal to kneel and pray in the Rotunda, and rather soon the capitol police were handcuffing us and transporting us to a holding pen and later to separate jail cells. The "we" were the national leaders of churches who opposed this war, men and women from national and regional church offices together with us less senior staff organizers.

For years the image has stuck with me of this long line of church officials (who were more often lined up to process into church services in full clerical regalia, but in this case were) moving in file, handcuffed like common criminals to be processed (finger-printed and stripped of all personal items) for an unknown time behind bars.

All agree that war is hell on earth. Even military leaders affirm this but believe they fight wars to make peace—thinking that violence is a necessary kind of peacemaking. And so warfare—hell on earth—continues year after year, century after century. There is little need to look for hell in the afterlife when here on earth war continues every day with its butchery and slaughter, lies, and madness. Nor is there a need to look in the afterlife for evil personified by ancient people as Satan and the devil. War is evil, period. It is here and now. So why do people who really believe war is hell still willingly fight wars?

In ancient and medieval times fighting wars was a way for aristocrats to prove their courage and skill, to test their masculinity. War was one of the reasons for being in "aristocratic empires." This is the name that John H. Kautsky, professor emeritus of political science at Washington University in St. Louis, gives to world leaders across the centuries. He writes,

> in agrarian economies [which were the only economies until the modern era] where aristocrats live off peasants, the former must control the latter. Aristocrats therefore compete for control of land and peasants, principally by means of warfare, and their governments serve chiefly the functions of fighting other aristocrats and of taxing peasants . . . [Aristocrats'] dual role [was] as exploiters and warriors.[1]

Clearly Rome was an aristocratic empire in Jesus' time and was ruled by a tiny fraction of the population—aristocrats who did no physical work. They lived to fight wars using peasant conscripts on the front lines of battlefields and to tax all peasants. However, Rome had begun to commercialize by building plantations and cities and selling cash crops. So Kautsky notes another motive for Rome's wars—the commercial objective of capturing prisoners to be sold as slaves. [That] "Roman landowners invested in large slave contingents to operate their estates shows that Rome had been subject to commercialization."[2] Yet he adds that, "commercialization merely modifies the aristocrats' behavior and thinking, it does not put an end to [the aristocracy as the ruling class]."[3]

Although remnants of aristocracies still exist (note the persistence of privileged royals who are still honored by commoners throughout the world), corporate money has replaced hereditary aristocratic blood as the dominant power ruling nations and waging wars today. Former U.S. President Eisenhower called this power the "Military Industrial Complex." However, we might adapt that title to the "Military Corporate Complex" as mega corporations are replacing industry. The logic for perpetual war goes like this: The politicians who sponsor wars depend

1. Kautsky, *The Politics of Aristocratic Empires*, 6.
2. Ibid., 282.
3. Ibid., 355.

on massive campaign contributions to be elected and stay elected. Extremely wealthy individuals and corporations have the money and lobbyists to buy politicians who support perpetual warfare that necessitates the war equipment, jobs, and personnel that, in turn, support and are supported by the wealthy individuals and corporations. The war system perpetuates itself.

Like the tiny number of aristocrats of Jesus' time, the modern corporate elite is above the law. Members of the elite write the laws through their lobbyists. They are "too big to fail or jail." They also get the tax codes written in their favor (Note the so-called "Bush tax cuts for the very wealthy.") to protect their wealth, and they are rarely held responsible for causing economic disasters such as the recent recession. So the rich get richer and the poor get poorer. The young and poor are largely the ones who actually fight the wars of the old and rich.

Thus the blessing of peacemakers in this Beatitude may seem quaint and unrealistic, given the way the ruling class (whether aristocracy or the corporate elite) profit from wars. But, as we will see in the second part of this book, there are many ways to resist the evils of warmaking successfully. However, we cannot count on mainline media to report successful peacemaking, because peacemaking is not as sensational as war mongering. So war dominates media reporting. Also, the media, along with politicians, depend on and are owned by war profiting corporations (e.g., NBC is owned by General Electric, a major defense contractor). These corporations hire hundreds of lobbyists to write and promote laws and budgets that maintain perpetual wars.

After our arrest in the capital rotunda, our church group spent only two days and one night in jail cells, but I learned how humiliating even such a brief time in jail can be. The police quickly rid me of my romantic notion of writing letters from prison like Martin Luther King, Jr. and Dietrich Bonheoffer. For they confiscated all pencils and pens, and all written or writing materials; they even took shoes laces, belts, and all metal objects.

Other inmates in their cells soon learned that many of us were clergy and cried out most of the night for our prayers for them. We obliged and even sang hymns. Of course, none of this stopped the war, but we did join a movement in which a critical mass eventually ended it, even as the next war was soon to break out in Afghanistan.

Fig 21: Blessed are the peacemakers,

they will be called children of God.

When I made this sculpture of a peacemaker, the war there had begun and our bombers were busy with their devastating business. Some of the first people to die from these bombings were four United Nations de-miners. They were locally trained Afghans who had the deadly task of defusing anti-personnel mines. The horrible irony of killing such heroic peacemakers struck me powerfully. So I researched the various land mines that are used worldwide (some costing as little as $3.00 each) and the process of defusing them. I put on display images of such mines above the de-miner on side one of this relief sculpture. The de-miner lies on his stomach in a marked off area and carefully removes the detonator of the buried land mine. The dark, empty space in the shape of a butterfly is a mine that looks like a toy and is easily mistaken by children as a plaything.

On the second side of the relief sculpture I show another parade, this time of mine victims, blinded and with missing limbs who, like the de-miner, suffer from this form of warring madness without end. Blessed are these and all peacemakers. They are God's children.

Part Two

Jesus' Wisdom on Nonviolence

14

Introduction

Jesus lived in a brutal time and place. He must have been aware of the crushing violence of the Roman occupation, for violence is how the Romans stayed in power and it was ever present to the conquered land of Jesus' people. Right from the beginning of Jesus' life, the Gospel of Matthew reports that Mary, Joseph, and the baby Jesus traveled to Egypt to avoid Herod's slaughter of all children less than two years of age in and around Bethlehem in an effort to kill Jesus (Matt 2:16). Whenever there was any threat to Roman rule, Roman soldiers descended on the people, slaughtered or enslaved them, and burned their villages. One of many examples of this was when Jews tried to throw off Roman rule after Herod died. In response, Josephus writes, a Roman general named Varus rounded up 2000 suspected rebels and crucified them.[1] Jesus was about four years old when Herod died, so even as a youngster he must have known that: 1) the domination of Rome was so degrading of their self respect and honor that it was intolerable; 2) the Roman military would crush any violent resistance; and 3) therefore, violent resistance was impossible. Yet, resistance was necessary for the soul of this subordinate people.

In this violent context how could Jesus live and teach resistance in such a way that the Jewish people would survive and maintain their self-respect and honor? The Romans would crush any violent resistance, but to submit to the Romans would destroy the will and soul of the people. What to do in such a traumatic environment of mass crucifixions, slaughter, and enslavement? What could Jesus teach and show a traumatized people to save them from this violence when some of their

1. Josephus, *Ant.*, 17.295; *War*, 2.75

own leaders were cooperating with Rome? How he responded to this impossible task is recorded in the gospels.

By looking at how Jesus responded to the political and economic realities of this time we can see how he worked out the meaning and methods of nonviolent resistance. This approach allows a conquered people to resist without violence and to preserve their self-respect and honor.

Nowadays we have a much more complete view of the many non-violent tactics used by subordinate people such as Jesus' audience. James C. Scott, quoted above, has laid out for us "the immense political terrain that lies between quiescence and revolt."[2] Scott calls this "vast terrain" a "continent" of actions concealed in the hidden transcripts of the subordinate groups. He uses Brer Rabbit stories as an example of the way subordinate slaves talked about tricking their slave masters. What is invisible to the dominant elite is like the infrared rays of the light spectrum that is ever present but invisible to normal vision. This hidden behavior that subordinate groups use to resist their overlords he calls "infrapolitics." We will explore examples of such infrapolitics and nonviolent actions in the gospels with the help of a biblical scholar, Richard Horsley.

Horsley sees Jesus as "one of those rare cases among popular leaders whose irrevocable declaration of the hidden transcript in condemnation of the dominate order constituted a political breakthrough that escalated into a broader movement.

The texts of Mark and Q are thus hidden transcripts that are the result of open political resistance that is highly unusual in peasant politics."[3] Indeed, Jesus was a nonviolent radical whose wisdom is found both in and between the lines of the gospels. Part two of this book spells out Jesus' wisdom on this nonviolent resistance that he taught with his sayings and actions.

2. Scott, *Domination*, 199.

3. Horsley, *Jesus in Context*, 183. I understand Horsley to mean that such *texts* are "highly unusual," not that *political resistance* was "highly unusual."

15

Jesus' Wisdom on Violence

"Those who take the sword will perish by the sword."

(Matt 26:47–53)

(Also Mark 14:43–50; Luke 22:47–53; John 18:1–11)

While he was still speaking, Judas, one of the twelve, arrived; with him was a large crowd with swords and clubs, from the chief priests and the elders of the people. Now the betrayer had given them a sign, saying, "The one I will kiss is the man; arrest him." At once he came up to Jesus and said, "Greetings, Rabbi!" and kissed him. Jesus said to him, "Friend, do what you are here to do." Then they came and laid hands on Jesus and arrested him. Suddenly, one of those with Jesus put his hand on his sword, drew it, and struck the slave of the high priest, cutting off his ear. Then Jesus said to him, "Put your sword back into its place; for all who take the sword will perish by the sword. Do you think that I cannot appeal to my Father, and he will at once send me more than twelve legions of angels?"

The wisdom of Jesus' saying on violence could hardly be clearer. Violence is not the way to live life either on a personal level or a public level.

The immediate context of this saying is Jesus' arrest at Gethsemane. A follower of Jesus resorts to violence to defend him with a sword and cuts off the ear of a slave. Jesus firmly rejects even this defensive violence and does the opposite of violence. He heals the ear of the slave.

Jesus' wisdom on nonviolence is consistent throughout the gospels, but he is by no means passive. He speaks and acts aggressively to heal, encourage, pray for, and support those who, like the slave, are at the bottom of the Roman social structure.

Although nonviolence is Jesus' clear response to violence, there are some passages that seem to say he actually favored the sword, the symbol of violence. Matthew 10:34b has Jesus say, "I have not come to bring peace but a sword," though in his parallel passage Luke quotes Jesus as saying "division" not "sword." "Do you think that I have come to bring peace to the earth? No, I tell you, but rather division" (Luke 12:51). Jesus indeed brought division, even division in households between parents and children and division between siblings (Luke 8:19–20; 12:52–53). Thus Luke and Matthew disagree. Is it a sword or division that Jesus brings in place of peace? When Matthew reports Jesus' words against the sword in Gethsemane, does that cancel out this reference to bringing not peace but a sword? And does Luke's report of "division" cancel out Matthew's "sword"? We have to choose. To my mind "division" fits better with the whole gospel story of Jesus bringing conflict against the corrupt world of his time with his rejection of violence in general, and with his teaching of nonviolent tactics. For Jesus never used or taught violence (sword), but he certainly divided people, even family members, and he used coercive force once in the temple when he overturned the moneychangers' tables and chased them out of the temple (John 2:13–17). Nevertheless, there is no record that he ever used a sword himself or physically injured any person in any way.

There is another debated passage in which Jesus is said to have told disciples to carry a sword along with a purse and knapsack. In Luke 22:36 he says. "The one who has no sword must sell his cloak and buy one." Later on, Luke's Jesus says that two swords are enough. (Crossan translates this phrase differently from the NRSV, as "Enough of that," which means Jesus rejects the swords just as he does in Gethsemane.[1]) If we follow the usual translation ("that is enough"), then this passage is directly opposed to Jesus' saying in Luke 9:3 and 10:4 where the disciples are told not to carry anything: "no staff, nor bag, nor bread, nor money," not even an "extra tunic."

Which of these sayings and translations should we follow when they appear to contradict each other? We have to decide. My best judg-

1. Crossan, *The Greatest Prayer*, 181.

ment is to follow Luke's use of the word "division" rather than Matthew's "sword" and the instruction to carry nothing, not even a sword. Christian tradition tells us that most of the disciples were martyred, not that they fought with a sword to their deaths, for using violence was wrong on principle and in practice.

The principle is that God's Empire is one of peace, justice, and love. There is no room for violence in this Empire, Jesus' ultimate goal. In practice, Rome had all the weapons and legions that were massive and expert in violence. They were trained and ready to put down any disruption to their rule. To use violence against them was suicidal. The Romans could easily respond to violent outbreaks with brutal retributions to set an example and deter future disturbances. Those they crucified they left hanging to discourage any thought of opposition to Roman rule. It is no great stretch to suggest that Rome would welcome a response of violence because Rome was well prepared for it. What Rome was not prepared for was Jesus' nonviolent tactics. That was what Jesus modeled the night he was arrested and throughout his ministry.

This sculpture depicts such nonviolent wisdom by Jesus covering the slaves' ear with his right hand and holding the blade of the sword with his left hand, preventing its use. He asserts the message that violence begets violence. The gospels report that he could have called down twelve legions of angels to protect him, but he does not use violence, not even to protect himself.

Sadly only a few people such as Martin Luther King, Jr. and Mahatma Gandhi have seriously followed Jesus' nonviolent teachings. When it comes to world powers dealing with major conflicts, King and Gandhi have been honored but largely ignored. Yet successful nonviolent uprisings include the recent ones in Eastern Europe, Egypt, and Tunisia, as well as older ones in India, the Philippines, and South Africa.

Live/Die by the Sword

16

Jesus' Wisdom on Militarism

"Wherever the corpse is, there the vultures [eagles] will gather."

(Matt 24:28; also Luke 17:37)

Corpse—Eagles

THIS WISDOM SAYING IS full of ambiguity, but it makes sense from a political perspective. First, the translation of *aetoi* in the NRSV and other translations is rendered as "vulture" rather than "eagles." Although both are possible, "eagle" is clearly a political translation, for the eagle was a sacred symbol for Rome and was to be protected in battle like a national flag or standard.

My view is that "eagle" is a better translation. Though vultures do indeed naturally gather around corpses as scavenger birds, Jesus and the gospel writers were not naturalists and were not primarily concerned to make everday observations about birds. Rather, Jesus in this saying is opposing the violence of Rome by calling attention to that violence.[1]

The second ambiguity of the saying is the term for "gather" or "will be gathered together" as in "the eagles gather" or "the eagles will be gathered." This Greek verb for gather, *sunachthēsontai,* is ambiguous for it can be translated as active ("eagles will gather") or passive ("eagles will be gathered"). Warren Carter translates this word as "will be gathered" in the latter, passive tense and suggests that the "scene depicts destroyed Roman troops ("the corpse") with fallen eagle standards scattered among them."[2] This passive translation fits Carter's view of Matthew as one who predicts the fall of Rome and "the final salvation of 'his people from their sins' [which] means the establishment of God's sovereignty or authority over heaven and earth [Matt] 28:18)."[3]

A political interpretation would clearly tilt toward an "eagle" translation of *áetoí* rather than the usual "vulture." However, a political translation of *sunachthēsontai* could be either passive (as Carter suggests) or active. Either way they are symbols of violence and death *by* Rome or of the death *of* Rome.

This image of a corpse in the foreground of the sculpture suggests the active translation, "will gather." The soldiers gather with the eagle on their shields, poles, and in the emblem of SPQR (*Senatus Populusque Romanus,* The Senate and People of Rome). One is grinning with his active sword in hand. He and the others are hardly heroic warriors, yet they are definitely strongly associated with violence and death. Matthew's Jesus does not see these agents of Roman brutality in a good light. They are quite the opposite: agents of Satan and evil who are condemned for their colonial domination.

1. See Warren Carter for an exhaustive analysis of the biblical usages of "eagle" and "vulture" in "Are there Imperial Texts in this Class?," 467–87.

2. Carter, *Matthew and Empire,* 87.

3. Ibid.

However, this negative view of Roman militarism is not universal. When I sought out images of Roman soldiers on the web so that I could draw and sculpt their uniforms accurately, I discovered that even today men periodically dress up in these Roman uniforms and presumably are proud to march around reenacting Roman formations. Luke's Jesus seems to see beyond the uniforms to the individual people who wear them when he healed the certurion soldier's slave and commended his faith (Luke 7:1–10). Yet, healing a slave and commending a soldier's faith is not the same as endorsing militarism or slavery. Even though Jesus has been represented as blessing militarism throughout western history and even of being a warrior himself, this could not be farther from his life and teachings. His typical greeting was not a military salute but the blessing "Peace be with you."

17

Steps Out of the Cycle of Violence: Negotiation

"Point out the fault when the two of you are alone."

(Matt 18:15; also Luke 17:3)

"If another member of the church sins against you, go and point out the fault when the two of you are alone. If the member listens to you, you have regained that one."

THIS WISDOM IS THE first of four steps Matthew proposed to the early church to deal with conflicts. Since it was addressed to the church that developed long after Jesus lived, scholars agree it is Matthew speaking rather than Jesus. Matthew is likely adapting words from Q because a similar phrase is present in Luke 17:3. The wisdom of speaking directly and alone to the offending party is well-proven wisdom in psychology, sociology, and peace studies. It is clearly in the spirit of Jesus if not his exact words. Jesus and Matthew know that it is wiser to confront a person in private than in public. The social scientist, James C. Scott says, "What is reasonably clear, however, is that any indignity is compounded greatly when it is inflicted in public . . . [C]onsider . . . the difference between a dressing down . . . an employee may receive from his boss in the privacy of the boss's office and the same dressing down delivered before all of the employee's peers and subordinates."[1]

Once I saw this wisdom in action during a common meal at a work camp I attended. Our group leader could have corrected my friend in front of the whole group of twenty work group members at dinner. But

1. Scott, *Domination*, 113.

he waited until dinner was over. My friend usually left food on his plate after the meals ended, and this was unacceptable, especially since we were building housing for refugees who often had little to eat. The work group leader observed my friend's plate with leftover food and decided to confront him directly and alone.

The obvious reason that direct and private confrontation is wise is that it gets to the source of the problem and avoids the distortions that are common when others are involved. Miscommunications can be cleared up much more easily in private. Also, if the two parties are alone, the confrontation is less embarrassing to the offending party. If direct and private confrontation clears up the offence, "you have regained that one"—that is, you have restored the friendship and settled the dispute.

However, it is more often the case that when a person is offended, the last person he or she wants to talk to or be alone with is the offender. Our group leader might have been tempted to ignore the problem or to confront my friend within the whole group rather than privately. Within the whole group the leader might feel safer, could use the confrontation as a deterrent to warn others not to waste food, and could display his authority. But my friend surely would have been embarrassed. It is likely he would have wanted to retaliate in some way. Then the conflict might have spiraled out of control. Or if the confrontation is avoided, the problem could fester beneath the surface and explode later. Matthew's wisdom, therefore, goes against our natural tendency to avoid confronting an offender directly and in private. Yet, that wisdom is clearly the most effective, and most likely to succeed in resolving a conflict.

Negotiate Directly and Alone

"Negotiation" is the modern term for this two-party, direct encounter. Our group leader called my friend aside and, when they were alone, calmly affirmed him and complimented the work he had been doing. Then he explained how poor and hungry the refugees were and how we work groupers needed to exemplify concern for their plight in other ways besides building homes for them. That included how we conserved our food and ate all that we put on our plates. My friend understood the reasons for cleaning his plate and he even thanked the group leader for his diplomacy. He realized that he could have been warned in the presence of the whole group or been judged as greedy or careless or slyly put down with satire or sarcasm. All of these approaches would have embarrassed my friend and even tempted him to respond negatively to the leader in some way. By contrast, our leader's wisdom was effective and helpful. For he had used the wisdom in Matthew by speaking directly and alone to my friend, and in return my friend cleaned his plate at every meal during the rest of the work camp.

This story is a tiny dispute compared to international conflicts, but national governments have generally not learned this simple principle of direct, nonviolent confrontation. Often their first response to a conflict is to withdraw their ambassadors and cut off all direct contact with their adversary. For example, as of this writing, Israel and the Palestinian Authority are refusing to talk to each other over the issues of Israel building housing for their settlers on Palestinian land, the return of Palestinian refugees, and firm guarantees of Israel's defenses and other issues.

18

Steps out of the Cycle of Violence: Mediation

"Take one or two others along with you."

(Matt 18:16; also Luke 17:3)

"But if you are not listened to, take one or two others along with you, so that every word may be confirmed by the evidence of two or three witnesses."

THIS WISDOM OF BRINGING a witness or two to help settle a dispute is an amazingly practical and biblical means of nonviolent conflict resolution. Today witnesses are called mediators and are impartial guides in a conflict resolution process who confirm "every word." This second step of mediation follows negotiation (or step one) when direct and private confrontation does not work.

Mediation is widely used in labor disputes, international diplomacy, marital fights, and church conflicts. Even elementary schools have adopted mediation techniques for settling playground dust-ups nonviolently. Mediation is a process of guiding adversaries through steps of communication when emotions are high. It requires special training for a mediator to deal with these strong emotions. The mediator has to maintain a calm demeanor and convince the disputing parties that she/he is sufficiently impartial and competent to be trusted to move the conflict from being a battle to win to a problem to solve. Instead of attacking each other, the mediator leads the parties into attacking the problem to be solved.

Briefly, the mediation process is as follows:

Both parties must air their grievances without the other party's interruption and with equal amount of time assured by the mediator.

The mediator listens very carefully in order to be able to define precisely the issues(s) involved and the basic interests of each party. Then he/she renames those issues and interests in neutral or "laundered language." Once the rhetoric and emotions are reduced, those basic issues and interests are often not as conflictual as the parties initially assumed. Then the mediator guides the parties to create their own solutions to these issues so that the basic interests of each are met as much as possible, or at least to a level that each can live with. The mediator draws up an agreement which the two parties sign which specifies who will do what and when to accomplish the steps in the agreement. Then strict enforcement by an authorized person or persons is essential.

One example of such mediation is the work of George J. Mitchell, a former senator from Maine, who mediated the long-lasting wars between Protestants and Catholics in Northern Ireland. This successful mediation is called the "Good Friday Agreement" as it was finalized on Good Friday, 1998, the day when peace finally came to Northern Ireland. The agreement that Mitchell mediated was between Protestants (led by Ian Paisley, who wanted Northern Ireland to remain a part of Britain) and Catholics (led by *Sinn Fein,* who wanted total independence from Britain and unification of Northern Ireland with the Irish Republic. This battle had gone on since 1690, and periodically exploded into violence that came to be called "the troubles." With patient leadership and many months of mediation, Mitchell was able to broker a power sharing arrangement that has held ever since.[1]

Jimmy Carter likewise mediated the battle between Israel and Egypt in what is called the "Camp David Accords" hammered out over thirteen days at the Camp David retreat. These two countries have been at war since the time of Moses and the Pharaohs. The peace agreement has held since March, 1997.[2]

In these and many other mediations, the techniques very briefly summarized above were used successfully. Yet few people are aware of these successes because the news media thrive on reporting conflicts that are raging, not on peace-making.

Closer to home, a local church asked me as a trained mediator to mediate a conflict, and I accepted the invitation. The conflict was this: the church's deacons were supposed to tend to the many aspects of the worship services and care giving together with the pastor. But virtually

1. Mitchell, *Making Peace.*
2. Carter, *Talking Peace*, 3–20.

all cooperation between them had ended. One deacon had resigned because he said the pastor had undermined him, and the rest of the deacons were about to follow suit. The pastor was in a deep funk, feeling completely unappreciated and undermined by the deacons. He had begun to update his ministerial profile and plan his departure. There was gossip around the church about finding his replacement.

I was asked to give the relationship one last try by mediating the dispute. It took three two-hour sessions to go through the mediation process. In it the pastor and deacons aired their concerns, paraphrased each other's feelings, and worked out ten issues that needed to be addressed. By the third session they had agreed on ten actions, mainly to deal with the poor communications between the pastor and deacons. These actions were sent to the church council to ratify and implement.

I made a point of attending the next few council meetings to make sure the council did not drop the ball as often happens. Sure enough the first council agenda only had four of the ten action recommendations listed. I insisted that all ten be dealt with, and they were. I continued to follow the implementation of these actions and even threatened to bring in Rocky Balboa from near-by Philadelphia to help enforce them. Of course, I was bluffing but I was determined to see the mediation work, and it did.

Mediation.

19

Steps Out of the Cycle of Violence: Arbitration

"Tell it to the church [assembly]." "If the member refuses to listen to them [the witness or mediator], tell it to the church [assembly]."

(Matt 18:17a)

THE NEW DIVISION HEAD arrived at the company promising his board of directors that he would turn the company around, making it more productive. After a few months on the job, the division head selected ten employees and told them one by one that they were no longer needed and would not receive severance pay for their work at the company. When the employees asked why they were being fired, he would only say that he had decided to proceed this way, which was not a satisfying answer to the ten. He did not seem to feel he owed them a reason for firing them or denying them any severance pay. It quickly became clear that no negotiation was possible. He refused to talk about the firings. The ten were simply to pack up and leave. What could they do nonviolently to oppose this firing without severance? Were verbal attacks on the one hand or quiet surrender on the other the only options?

There is a third step when negotiations and mediation do not work: arbitration. In his gospel Matthew says that when a direct and private approach (negotiation) does not work, and when calling in witnesses (mediation) does not work either, then we are to "tell it to the church [*ecclesia* or assembly]." That is the responsible body (in this case, the board of directors) that had final say on all matters of the company. Why are these steps important?

First, it is important to go through these steps because they deal directly with the dispute rather than surrendering or attacking. They are nonviolent in every way, and the dispute is taken to the whole assembly only when negotiation and mediation do not work. Quite frequently, however, people do not have the patience to keep at this task. So they attack their adversary from a safe distance, or threaten to sue, or quietly submit to their adversary's demands. They "cave in" and then regret it. Yet with patience and determination one can usually press for a fair or better resolution of the dispute by telling the whole assembly and seeking a mandatory judgment or arbitration.

In the ancient times of the First Testament, it was the king or his agents who arbitrated disputes, not a board of directors or an assembly. Perhaps the most familiar example is Solomon's arbitration of a dispute between two women who both claimed to be the mother of a child. The king ordered a sword and said, "Divide the living boy in two; then give half to one, and half to the other." One woman agreed and the other said, "Please, my lord, give her the living boy; certainly do not kill him!" Solomon decided that the woman who begged him to spare the child must be the true mother and gave her the boy (1 Kings 3:16–28).

In our earlier example, the ten fired employees organized and consulted a lawyer who proposed a mediation process again that was quickly dismissed by the division head. Then the ten discovered that the company had a grievance procedure that none had ever heard about before the firing. That procedure allowed for a hearing before the board of directors. So they took the next step and asked for a place on the agenda of the next board of directors' meeting. They told this assembly that the firing of the ten was unjust, that no explanation was ever given for it, and that severance pay had been denied them. The board heard their protest and, with a split vote, backed the new division head on his decision to fire the ten. However, they affirmed the employees' request for severance pay. That amounted to one month's pay for every year of employment. This would allow the ten some help as they looked for new jobs.

Telling the whole assembly/board was an example of the third step of arbitration. The board's decision was final and no further appeal was possible. The severance pay was helpful as the ten employees departed the company.

What could the employees have done if an even less satisfactory solution had been arbitrated? What if no severance had been granted?

Could they then at least use verbal violence? Or should they then have given up? That calls for step four, to which we turn next.

Arbitration

20

Steps Out of the Cycle of Violence: Letting Go

"If the offender refuses to listen even to the church [assembly], let such a one be to you as a Gentile and a tax collector."

(Matt 18:17b)

One of my friends lives with the ghost of his failure when his company went bankrupt. Another friend who used to keep us entertained for hours with his great stories lost his standing as a minister and now talks mostly about how he was mistreated by the authorities years ago. Another friend yearns for a chance to set the record straight with a person who claimed the friend lied about him, but he will not talk to that person. All of these folks are haunted by their past conflicts like Dickens's Scrooge in *A Christmas Carol.* They have an unhealthy attachment to the pain and sorrow they have suffered and will not let it go.

The ancient people of biblical times would say that these friends of mine have demons, or better, that the demons have them. That unhealthy attachment (addiction) or demon of one's past conflicts is a very powerful force even though it has no existence apart from the person's imagination and memory.

When we try to resolve a conflict and yet fail to negotiate, mediate, or arbitrate it, then we must take the next step and let it go. Matthew makes this point in an odd way. He tells us to let a person who will not respond to the first three steps to "be to you as a Gentile and a tax collector." The meaning seems clear enough: "Let it go. Do not spend any more energy on this conflict."

However, the negative reference to Gentiles and tax collectors is odd because in fact Jesus did not reject tax collectors or Gentiles. He is quoted as saying that "the tax collectors and prostitutes are going into the kingdom of God ahead of you [Pharisees]" (Matt 21:31). In addition, Matthew himself is said to have been a tax collector in Matthew 10:3 and 9:9. As for Gentiles, Paul, who wrote his letters at least thirty years before Matthew's Gospel, saw his mission as being to and for the Gentiles ("Inasmuch then as I am an apostle to the Gentiles. . . ." Rom 11:13).

The fourth step of Matthew's approach to dealing with conflict is important because letting go of failure, an argument, or a fight with a person who will not respond to the first three steps is necessary for one's own spiritual well being. Otherwise these demons of past conflicts will destroy one's soul. Or to put it in psychological language, an unhealthy attachment or addiction to past adversity and conflicts is psychologically damaging.

So far this discussion has seemed to apply mostly to individual's spiritual struggles. But the wisdom of letting go of a conflict when all reasonable efforts have been tried also applies to large groups of people, nations, and ethnic and religious groups. And there is a long list of these groups that harbor centuries of hatred of others: Protestants and Catholics in Ireland, Sunnis and Shiites in Iraq, Muslims and Catholics in Bosnia, Tutsis and Hutus in Uganda, Jews and Arabs in Palestine, Arabs in Northern Sudan and Christians in Southern Sudan, and many others. They simply will not or cannot let go.

The old cliché, "Let go and let God," contains some helpful wisdom. For harboring the unresolved conflicts and wars of the past accomplishes nothing; it simply eats away at the soul of a nation or an individual. Letting go is the opposite of getting revenge. Yet some people and groups live for revenge, and popular films and television programs thrive on revenge because it promises to satisfy our righteous anger. But is revenge a wise motive by which to live? The word "revenge" occurs only twice in the Bible (Prov 6:34 and Jer 20:10) and then it is presented as the unwise behavior of a jealous husband and of Jeremiah's persecutors. The Bible instead counsels us to let go of adversity so it will let go of us.

The often-quoted prayer of Reinhold Niebuhr calls for us to accept things that cannot be changed. That is the same as letting go of unchangeable things. An unresolved conflict is such an unchangeable thing we must let go. The prayer goes like this: God, give us grace to accept with serenity the things that cannot be changed, courage to change the things that should be changed, and the wisdom to distinguish the one from the other."

Letting Go

Past conflicts are unchangeable, but we can change our attitude toward them. Jesus' wisdom frees us to let go of them and live abundantly in the present and for the future. "The wisdom to distinguish the one from the other" is what this book is about.

21

Tactics to Preserve Dignity and Resist Oppression

Retaliation or Turning the Other Cheek
"Turn the other cheek."

(Matt 5: 39b; also Luke 6:29a)

"You have heard that it is said, 'An eye for an eye
and a tooth for a tooth.' But I say to you,
do not resist an evildoer. But if anyone strikes you
on the right cheek, turn the other also . . ."

I DOUBT THAT ANY saying of Jesus has been misunderstood and misused more than this one to "turn the other cheek." The clearest illustration I know of its true meaning is a story told by Ian Frazier of a Lakota girl named SuAnne Big Crow from the Pine Ridge Reservation in South Dakota.[1] She was a super athlete especially in basketball and was elevated to the varsity team when she was only fourteen. She played for the Lady Thorpes, so named after the great Sac and Fox, Olympic athlete, Jim Thorpe. Her older cousin, Doni, was captain of the basketball team.

They were playing another high school team at Lead, a town in western South Dakota. The gymnasium was filled with white fans from Lead who taunted the Lakota girl's team with fake Indian sounds as they lined up between the locker room and the basketball court before the game began. The small gym in Lead made the noise of fans seem much

1. Frazier, *On the Rez*, 205–9.

louder than usual. The high school band joined in with a tom tom beat as the fans teased the Pine Ridge team with hand to mouth "wah, wah, wah" imitations.

SuAnne's cousin, Doni, was supposed to lead the Lady Thorpes onto to the court for pre-game warm ups. She stood at the head of the team with the ball without moving as the mocking noise grew louder and louder. Finally, the mocking got to her and she turned around and said, "I can't do this." Very quickly SuAnne took the ball from her and started to lead the team out. Doni said, "Now don't you embarrass us." SuAnne led the team on to the court single file with the coach bringing up the rear. Suddenly she stopped in mid court. The team members bumped into each other, even the coach. What she did then was to stand up against the mocking crowd in a unique act of nonviolent resistance. She "turned the other cheek."

However, what she did next was not the popular interpretation of turning the other cheek which has come to mean, "absorb insults, give in, cave, be a door mat," that is, passive non-resistance. Nothing could be farther from Jesus' meaning of this wisdom saying. For none of the gospels report Jesus being passive or preaching surrender to mocking insults or a slap on the cheek. On the contrary, he constantly and aggressively challenged people, especially people in power. (To be sure he was mostly silent before Pilate, but that was a defiant silence that refused to buy any of Pilate's claims or assumptions about God or Rome's empires.)

What SuAnne did exemplified Jesus' nonviolent resistance that is not passive resistance or passive non-resistance. Clearly, Jesus was nonviolent, but he always stood up to and actively resisted evil and violence.

"Stand up," "stand against," "take a stand" is what "resist" (in Greek, *antistenai*) means. Thus, unlike the NRSV translation and other translations of this passage, recent scholars translate "resist" as "Do not react *violently* against the one who is evil." *Antistenai* is a military term meaning to stand and fight against a foe. We are not to use violence when we, nevertheless, take a stand and react to violence against us such as a slap on the cheek. We are to react as Jesus did and respond to violence with non-violence. Of course, we are to resist evildoers, but without violence. How so?

What could this turning the other cheek mean if it is not to be submissive, to take it on the chin (or cheek), not to fight back when struck on the right cheek? Luke leaves out the word "right" and only says, "If anyone strikes you on the cheek, offer the other also" (6:29).[2] New Testament scholar, Walter Wink, has untangled this saying and even developed role playing skits to act out its meaning.[3] Wink reminds us of the hierarchical social structure of Jesus' time in which a dominant person (for example, a master of slaves) would only backhand a lower-class person or slave and then only with his right hand, as the left hand was reserved for purposes of hygiene. The backhand slap was meant to hurt and to humiliate, to degrade the slapped person and put him/her in his/her place in the social pyramid.

As it turns out, it is impossible to back hand (using the right hand) a person's left ("other") cheek. A backhand slap is a weapon of humiliation to keep the social hierarchy in place, whereas a right-handed punch would assume equality of the slave and master. And the major point of the backhand was to deny that equality and make sure the slave stayed subservient to the master. Thus, when the slave "turns the other cheek," he or she is saying with this gesture, "You cannot take away my honor and self respect even if you slap me."

By advising his audience of dominated people to "turn the other cheek," Jesus is giving them a nonviolent tactic that stands up to the dominant master, throws him off guard, and cleverly asserts the dominated slave's dignity and self respect.[4] This is one of many examples of reactions one can use to resist the domination of an oppressor but to resist without violence.

Now back to the basketball game in South Dakota: at mid court, SuAnne Big Crow removed her warm up jacket, draped it around her shoulders like a shawl, and began singing a Lakota song and dancing the shawl dance she had learned at pow wows as a little girl. The Lead fans and even her teammates were dumbfounded. The thunderous mocking stopped. Suddenly all got quiet. Only her song could be heard. She continued to sing and dance amid the eerie silence. Finally, respectful applaud began, and gradually the fans rose to their feet with appreciative

2. Although Luke's version of this saying does not mention the right cheek as Matthew does, turning the other cheek would still be an act of nonviolent defiance of the master's backhand.

3. Wink, *The Powers That Be*, 101–3.

4. If this interpretation seems odd to those new to it, Wink is not alone in suggesting it. See also Crossan, *The Essential Jesus*, 164 and Carter, *Matthew and Empire*, 142.

clapping for SuAnne's amazing performance. She had turned the other cheek. The Lady Thorpes went on to win the game.[5]

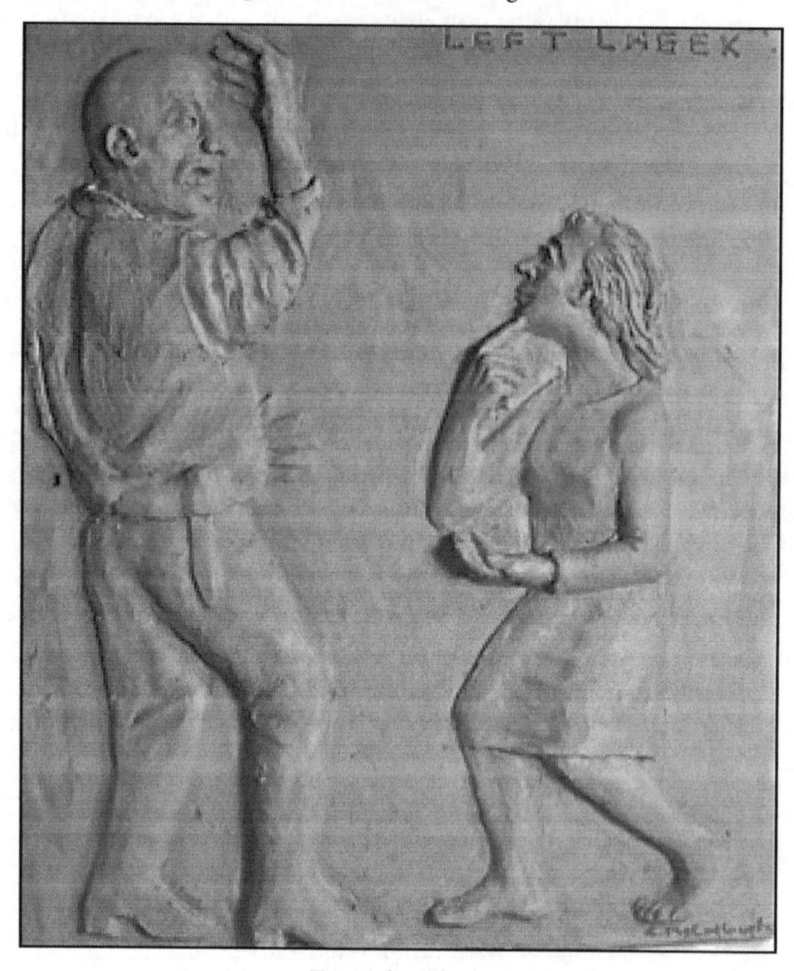

Turn Other Cheek

5. I told this story at the Eagle Butte Learning Center on the Cheyenne River Lakota Reservation and asked if anyone of these Lakota people had heard it before. Some had heard it, and one woman who confirmed all these details said she was present at the game where all this happened. I was pleased to learn that the story was thus witnessed as true in every detail.

22

Tactics to Preserve Dignity and Resist Oppression

Give Your Cloak as Well

"If anyone wants to sue you and take your coat, give your cloak as well."

(Matt 5:40; also Luke 6:29b)

In Nigeria, international oil companies such as Chevron/Texaco found great oil deposits and have been pumping it out and profiting from its sale. However, in doing so, they have fouled the environment and have not put their vast riches back into local villages, many of which do not even have electricity. How could poor Nigerians go up against mega corporations and expect to get jobs or any improvement in their environment? The cards were stacked against them, so maybe they could not. But a number of women (wives and mothers of would-be workers) refused to let the corporations continue to take their land's natural resources and give little back. What influence, power, or weapons did they have with which to go up against such powerful international oil companies? They had no money, no lawyers, no political clout. Things seemed to be rigged against the women as well as their men.

The poor people Jesus came to serve were equally powerless—or so they thought. But Jesus advised that when a creditor comes to sue you and take your coat, give your cloak as well.

In order to translate this into modern perspectives we need to know that in Jesus' time, first, a creditor could take a debtor to court and demand all of a debtor's assets; second, a greedy enough creditor could even sue a debtor for his clothing, such as his coat; and third, back then men usually wore only two garments—an outer coat and an inner cloak, but no underwear as we do in our time.

These economic conditions illustrate one more way the poor were exploited by the greed of the wealthy. Jesus not only took a stand against the direct violence of Rome and its collaborators but against the indirect violence of economic exploitation. How? Since violent resistance was not only wrong but futile, Jesus' wisdom calls for another clever, non-violent tactic. He said that when you are taken to court for your coat, give your cloak too (leaving you naked). This will so shame the creditor for his greed that the naked debtor will retain his honor. In this way the naked debtor would take the initiative by standing up against the extortion of the creditor and the whole economic system.

The women of Nigeria came up with a similar tactic of non-violent resistance. They organized and went to the huge Eseravos terminal of Chevron/Texaco. They detained the workers at the terminal and then, as we read, "unarmed village women holding 700 Chevron Texaco workers inside a southeast Nigeria oil terminal . . . threatened a traditional and powerful shaming gesture . . . removing their own clothes." One of the women's leaders explained this embarrassing but non-violent action this way. "Our weapon is our nakedness," said Helen Odeworitse, a representative for the villagers in the extraordinary week-old protest for jobs, electricity and development in Nigeria's oil-rich Niger Delta."[1] The women eventually won concessions for most of their demands from the oil companies.

1. "Nigerian Women Threaten Nude Protest," Associated Press news release, July 14, 2002. *New York Times*. "Nigerian Women, in Peaceful Protest, Shut Down Oil Plant," July 14, 2002.

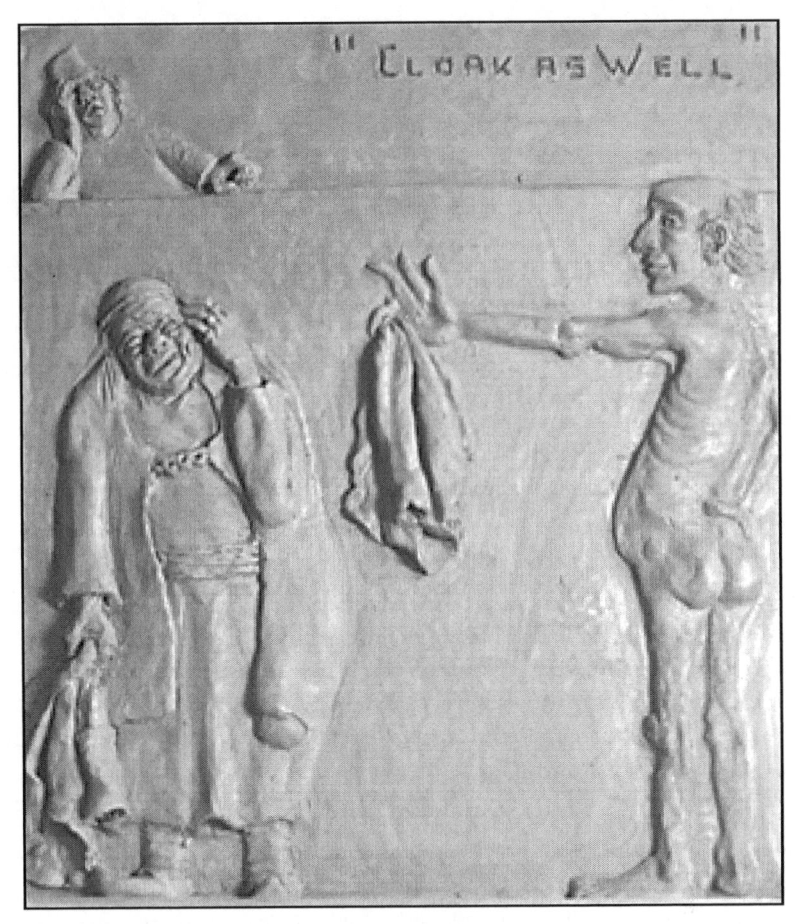

Cloak as Well

To say that the weak and poor are powerless is not correct. There are many things like this nakedness that can be used as a weapon against domination and greed. James C. Scott has written an extensive book that names *The Weapons of the Weak: Everyday Forms of Peasant Resistance*, focused on poor villages in southeast Asia. Gene Sharp likewise has listed hundreds of successful nonviolent acts of resistance from around the world in his three-volume work, *The Politics of Nonviolent Action*. In saying "give your cloak as well," Jesus reminds us that the weak and poor do have power but need imagination to find successful tactics of nonviolent resistance to win the justice they deserve. Of course, this act of nakedness is only one example of what can be done against extortion and a reminder that there are many other creative and nonviolent tactics.

23

Tactics to Preserve Dignity and Resist Oppression: Go Also the Second Mile

"And if anyone forces you to go one mile, go also the second mile."
(Matt 5:41)

THIS SAYING GIVES JESUS' wisdom on how to respond to being forced to work for others without compensation. Being forced to carry someone else's burden is not the same as volunteering to help someone. But refusing to do so to a violent bully may not be wise. However, one can respond without refusing to carry the burden, without resorting to violence, and without surrendering one's self respect. The same can be done to respond to threats, stealthy intimidations, bullying, and hate violence.

In 1993 virtually the whole town of Billings, Montana rose up in this way to resist the threats of the KKK and Neo Nazis. The hate activities of these groups began with leafleting the cars of people who were attending a Martin Luther King, Jr. birthday celebration. Then the groups overturned tombstones at a Jewish cemetery and painted swastikas on the home of Dawn Fast Horse along with these threatening words, "Die Indian Die." Individuals began to help the victims of these attacks, but it took a final threat to motivate the whole community to action. That was when a piece of cinder block came crashing through the window of a Jewish family that was displaying an image of a Menorah for Hanukkah. What could the people of Billings do to stop these attacks on the minority members of their community?

Going the second mile is a helpful biblical response to such violence if we know the context of this wisdom saying. Otherwise, it is misused, just as the 'turn the other cheek' saying is misused to encourage masochistic responses to violence. In Jesus' time Roman soldiers were allowed to draft their colonial subjects to carry their equipment for one mile, but not more than one mile. Thus, when Jesus said, "Go the second mile" when you are forced to carry a burden one mile, he is offering another assertive, but nonviolent, response to bullies who force things on subject people. By going the second mile one preserves one's self-respect, takes the initiative from the soldier, and makes him go against the rules. The burden carrier does not threaten the soldier; he simple overdoes the forced command.

Again, Jesus' wisdom teaches creative nonviolent resistance to Roman domination. This example says, "You can make me do your work because you have the power to do so and can use violence against me with impunity. But you cannot defeat my self-regard. 'Carry your gear a mile? I'll carry it two miles.'"

Back in Billings, Montana, after the window of the house with the Menorah was smashed, the churches, other civic groups, and the police chief got together along with the local newspaper staff, *The Billings Gazette,* to try to stop these violent threats. They came up with the idea of placing pictures of the Menorah in windows all over the town. The newspaper printed a full-page picture of a Menorah and asked people to display it for all to see, particularly for the KKK and Neo Nazis. Over 10,000 people did so and the hate threats stopped, and no serious acts of hate violence have occurred since.

Go the Second Mile.

The Billings community did not simply express its regret that some minority people were attacked. Rather, they went the second mile and risked themselves and their property by joining with the Jewish family's display of the Menorah. Ten thousand Menorahs in windows offered the hate groups plenty of targets. Like taking a forced burden a second mile, the Billings community overdid the targets of the hate groups and so ended the group's violent threats nonviolently.

24

Seeing Peace

"If you . . . had only recognized . . .
the things that make for peace!"

"As he came near and saw the city, he wept over it, saying "If you, even you, had only recognized on this day the things that make for peace!'"

(Luke 19:41–42)

I REMEMBER EXACTLY WHERE I was on 9/11/01 when the Twin Towers and Pentagon were attacked. I was at Andover Newton Theological School near Boston as resident artist. It was the first day of classes, but none were held, only a mournful worship service. Soon after, the student association asked me to create a memorial sculpture to what we lost that day. It would be their gift to the seminary to be set up on the campus. My first thought was of the fourteen Stations of the Cross that are in many Catholic Churches. But I moved away from that idea after reading Daniel Berrigan's book[1] on those Stations which pointed out their origin in the crusades. My work had to be about peace, not war. The Stations of the Cross start with the trial of Jesus and end with his entombment. Instead, I proposed to make fourteen scenes depicting Jesus from his entry into Jerusalem to his trial. Many of these scenes show his nonviolent wisdom. The student association agreed, so I began. Now all fourteen pieces hang on the wall of the academic building at the seminary where I hope they visually inspire students preparing for ministry.

1. Berrigan, Parker, *Stations*, vii-xiii.

The first sculpture in the fourteen is of Jesus' Entry. It compares a peaceful donkey ride to a pompous warhorse strutting into the city. There is no wisdom saying with it, but the visual scene clearly communicates that violence is not the way. The second scene has Jesus crying over that city and groaning this saying "If you . . . had only recognized the things that make for peace."

Cry for Peace

I will spell out here four of these fourteen images that illustrate Jesus' wisdom on nonviolent things that make for peace. I have displayed other images from this series to illustrate other aspects of Jesus' wisdom teachings.

This saying on the things that make for peace is only in Luke, but the entry into Jerusalem that immediately precedes it in Luke is reported in all four gospels: Luke 19:28–40; Mark 11:11; Matt 21:1–11; and John 12:12–15; see also Zach 9:9 and Psalm 118:26. Jesus' entry on a donkey is a mocking dramatization of what does *not* make for peace. So we ask again the question, "This . . . as opposed to what?" What are those things that do not make for peace? What is it that is hidden from our eyes that the people of Jerusalem, (the city's name means "God's peace,") could not see? By telling the story of Jesus' entry into Jerusalem on a donkey, the gospel writers are comparing his comical parade to the usual grandiose display of power when a king, general, or governor enters a city on a warhorse or chariot, surrounded by threatening guards and frightening weapons. Such parades have continued into our time and are obviously meant to warn everyone not to mess with the ruler in power or the "peace" he has imposed with his wars. In Jesus' time that peace was the *Pax Romana,* the Roman peace.

The gospel writers used the lines from Zachariah 9:9 to show a different, peaceful way to arrive in the city. ("Lo, your king comes to you; triumphant and victorious is he, humble and riding on a donkey. . . .") Thus Luke precedes this saying on peace with a theatrical stunt of a servant king on a peaceful donkey as opposed to a military conqueror on a warhorse. Instead of threatening guards and frightful weapons, this parade is accompanied by palm branches and cloak carpets of welcome. So we have Palm Sunday to this day. But Jesus, no doubt, would weep for us as well because we also put our faith in military might and give over $600 billion per year to it in the United States. The things that make for peace are also still hidden from our eyes.

Donkey Parade

All four gospels quote Psalm 118:26 ("Blessed is the one who comes in the name of the lord"). But only Luke leaves out "Hosanna," probably to soften the saying for his Roman audience. For "Hosanna" means "deliver us." Deliver us from what? Clearly the people of Jerusalem hoped to be delivered from Roman tyranny. The people naturally expected that delivery to come by violent acts of military might just as King David had done. But Jesus rejected this violence and war. He cried out for "the things that make for peace" and then went to the temple to teach those things that do make peace. But he saw that the temple itself had become a haven for thieves even though the thieves included the established high priests. They were corrupt, and they exploited the people.

In this sculpture Jesus is pushing over the pillars of the temple with one hand and with the other hand is pointing to the here and now as that place where God's empire is "in our midst."

Kingdom Here and Now

For the temple where God was supposed to be had become a "den of robbers." The temple was a slaughterhouse where daily sacrifices of oxen, sheep, birds, and other animals occurred. And it was a bank that stored the tithes, debt records, and offerings of the people. The moneychangers aided this effort by exchanging currency for such sacrifices. Jesus symbolically cleared this misuse of the temple and turned over the moneychangers' tables. In this image I have made the table out of the symbol of Enron that for our time represents the vast corruption of mega corporations. Thus, one of the first things that makes for peace is correcting the misuse of the houses of worship as a place that money can buy, and restoring it as a place in which to honor and teach about God as a God of peace, justice, and equality where all have enough to live. This is the beginning of what makes for peace.

Robbers' Den.

25

Communion Versus Disunion

"This is my body . . . This is my blood."

(Mark 14:17–24; also Matt 26:17–25, Luke 22:7–13, John 13:21–30, 1 Cor 11:23–26)

When it was evening, he came with the twelve. And when they had taken their places and were eating, Jesus said, "Truly I tell you, one of you will betray me, one who is eating with me." They began to be distressed and to say to him one after another, "Surely, not I?" He said to them, "It is one of the twelve, one who is dipping bread into the bowl with me. For the Son of Man goes as it is written of him, but woe to that one by whom the Son of Man is betrayed! It would have been better for that one not to have been born."

While they were eating, he took a loaf of bread, and after blessing it he broke it, gave it to them, and said, "Take; this is my body." Then he took a cup, and after giving thanks he gave it to them, and all of them drank from it. He said to them, "This is my blood of the covenant, which is poured out for many."

All Christians receive communion, though the forms and frequency for doing so vary considerably. Some receive it daily, others weekly, or monthly, or quarterly. In my church we have communion on the first Sunday of each month. People come forward and form a standing circle as deacons serve bread and tiny cups of wine and grape juice, your choice. Just as there are many names for this ritual feast, such as "Lord's Supper," "Last Supper," "Eucharist," and "Holy Communion," there are many understandings of it. Some see it as a causal routine, others as an act of magic, and others still hold many positions in between.

When I was challenged to make a sculpture of Communion or the Lord's Supper, I had to work very hard to come up with the most basic yet concrete image I could, hoping and praying that my study and inspiration would come out through the clay. What do the words, "This is my body . . . This is my blood" mean? It helped my understanding again to answer the question, "as opposed to what?" When I asked this question in the larger context of the politics and economics of Jesus' time, I came to a core meaning and then began to work it into clay. *Comm*-union is opposed to *dis*-union or conflict of the demonic and deadly kind. I realized that it also helped to contrast the bread and cup (that give us life) to the money and sword (that can bring emptiness and death). I also thought of what Jesus was doing as opposed to what Judas was up to—Jesus being the one remembered as the bringer of life, and Judas as the bringer of death. In this sculpture Jesus brings bread and the cup to the table, life. Judas brings a sword and a bag of money, death, and emptiness.

Sword or Bread.

We eat and drink the nourishment of Jesus—as opposed to what? As opposed to the symbols of emptiness (money) and death (sword) of which Judas reminds us. We "do this [receive the bread and cup] in remembrance of [Jesus]" because, unlike Judas, we seek to take in all of the life-giving things Jesus stood for.

It also helps to contrast what we know of Judas with Jesus. The gospels tell us he cut a deal with the chief priests (Mark 14:10) to betray Jesus. I portray their conspiracy as Judas with his handlers at a news conference.

Judas' Deal

But when we turn the sculpture around, we see the rotting in their backs that suggests their corruption. Matthew reports that the chief priests "paid him thirty pieces of silver" after Judas asked them, "What will you give me if I betray him to you?" (Matt 26:15). Luke adds that "Satan entered into Judas" and that he consented to taking the money (Luke 22:6) to betray Jesus. The chief priests needed a secret, night-time betrayal because they were afraid of a riot if he were arrested in the day time. The gospels tell us they planned to kill Jesus. Why?

We have to remember that the high priests were the political leaders of Judea along with Pilate. They were appointed by Rome and served Rome's interests. Jesus was causing trouble for Rome, and the high priests reasoned that it was better for one man to die than for him to cause an uproar that would bring Rome's crushing reprisals down on all of Judea. The high priest "Caiaphas was the one who advised . . . that it was better to have one person die for the people" (John 18:14b). We need not doubt where their loyalty lay, for the high priests said to Pilate, "We have no king but the emperor," when Pilate asked them, "Shall I crucify your king?" (John 19:15).

So Judas brought death to the life giver, Jesus. If the bread/body and the cup/blood that give us both physical and spiritual life are contrasted to symbols of sword/death and money/emptiness, then Communion is a radical ritual indeed compared to the disunion of the emptiness and death brought by Judas who was doing the bidding of the high priests who in turn were serving Rome.

By participating in this Communion ritual, we are saying "yes" to fulfillment and life but also "no" to emptiness and death. Money, of course, buys good and needed things, but the addictive pursuit of money is demonic. That addiction/demon led Judas to help kill Jesus, leaving Judas so empty he committed suicide, according to the gospels.

Kiss of Death

The sculpture I made of Judas is hollow, empty as shown in his kiss of death.

When I receive communion, I remember the fullness of life I am given as opposed to the death and emptiness from which I am delivered. I made this skater in bronze to express the joy and grace of this gift of the fullness of life and the release from death and emptiness.

Fullness.

26

This World of Violence

"My kingdom is not from this world."

(John 18:36; also Mark 15:1–5; Matt 27:11–14; Luke 23:1–4)

> Then Pilate entered the headquarters again, summoned Jesus, and asked him, "Are you the King of the Jews?" Jesus answered, "Do you ask this on your own, or did others tell you about me?" Pilate replied, "I am not a Jew, am I? Your own nation and the chief priests have handed you over to me. What have you done?" Jesus answered, "My kingdom is not from this world. If my kingdom were from this world, my followers would be fighting to keep me from being handed over to the Jews. But as it is, my kingdom is not from here." Pilate asked him, "So you are a king?" Jesus answered, "You say that I am a king. For this I was born, and for this I came into the world, to testify to the truth. Everyone who belongs to the truth listens to my voice." Pilate asked him, "What is truth?"
> (John 18:33–38).

Jesus' trial before Pilate has usually been interpreted in a way that leaves Pilate innocent of his order to have Jesus tortured and crucified. Such an interpretation has been convenient for those who wrongly want to "blame the Jews" for Jesus' death. It also ignores the political context of the whole violent rule of Rome's governor, Pilate. Pilate washes his hands to mime his innocence; Bible interpreters have often gone along with that ruse.

Jesus faced a ruthless tyrant who was the only person in Judea allowed to order Jesus' death—and he did. One example of many of Pilates' vicious acts is in Josephus' report. It is generally acknowledged that Josephus was an apologist for Rome. So when he is critical of Roman leaders, his words become more credible. He reported that Samaritans gathered in great numbers to ascend their holy Mount Gerizzim where they were supposed to find "saved vessels" left by Moses. They never made it. "Pilate prevented it . . . by seizing upon the roads with a great band of horsemen and footmen, who fell upon those that had gotten together . . ."[1] Josephus does not explain why Pilate attacked the Samaritans, but it is likely that any large gathering was a threat to Roman absolute rule, Pilate's main commitment. Large gatherings were not permitted.

But when other Samaritan leaders complained of the slaughter to Vitellius, "president of Syria . . . ordered Pilate to go to Rome, to answer before the emperor to the accusation of the Jews."[2] However, the Emperor Tiberius died before Pilate reached Rome. So he escaped. But that ended Pilate's rule in Judea. Vitellius' order to send Pilate to Rome to answer charges of vindictive savagery was highly unusual and confirms the ruthlessness of Pilate, who in other cases did not hesitate to murder when there was any perceived threat to his rule. For Rome expected absolute control at all costs. Slaughter, enslavement, and torture were common and were accepted by the ruling elite.

Jesus was just such a threat, and his trial brings into particular focus the opposition of two worlds or empires, the nonviolent Empire of God and the violent Empire of Rome. The clearest and most succinct summary of these two empires I have found is this extensive quotation from Warren Carter. (His references are from Matthew.)

> Hence in asking Jesus if his title is 'King of the Jews,' Pilate asks Jesus, 'Are you the head of the resistance?' The title charges Jesus with sedition against the empire and Caesar. The title encapsulates challenge, threat, conflict.
>
> Moreover, the term highlights the vast differences between Jesus and Pilate over notions of empire that have appeared in Jesus' teaching and praxis. As a king, Jesus rejects imperial staples such as violence (5:38–42; 26:52) and domination (20:25–28). He rejects the exploitation and oppressive ways of kings (6:29) and

1. Josephus, *Antiquities*, 18.4.85–88.
2. Ibid.

> the hoarding of wealth (6:24–34). He rejects triumphant celebrations of domination through military subjugation (21:1–11). Rather he prefers the way of meekness (21:5), service (20:28), and prayer for God's alternative empire marked by bread and forgiveness of debt (6:9–13). The empire that his words and actions have attested . . . differs significantly from Rome's in demonstrating inclusiveness not elite privilege, mercy not force, service not domination, wholeness not deprivation.[3]

These differences are so great that Jesus remains mostly silent in response to Pilate's questions, only saying "you say so" in the synoptic gospels when Pilate asks if Jesus is king. But John reports a bit more. John has Jesus saying, "My kingdom is not from this world. If my kingdom were from this world my followers would be fighting . . ." (John 18:36). Clearly, Jesus' world is one where fighting and violence have been overcome. It is a world that Pilate cannot begin to understand, and Jesus knows there is no way to make him do so. Jesus is "letting go" of the impossible. Yet he does not try to save himself or ask for mercy. He refuses to accept any of Pilate's assumptions or taunts. He does not buy into any of the Roman rule of violence and fear. By his silence he opposes all that Pilate stands for. I have depicted him in this sculpture with his head tilted, his eyes half-closed, and his lips turned down to suggest his weariness at the violent ways of this world.

Why is this history and Bible study important to us today? First, it is important to understand that Jesus' silence is not capitulation. He is defiant and courageous to the end. With Jesus as our model for our lives, we must try to find such courage to face our own bullies. Second, it is important not to downplay Pilate's ruthlessness or accept his innocence because otherwise it becomes too easy to overlook our own abuses of power and our own support (through taxes and votes) for violent solutions to conflicts. Our usual argument for violence is, "It's a mean world out there requiring violent solutions." We rarely even try nonviolence. Third, we cannot blame the Jews for Jesus' death. Only the Rome-appointed high priests sought his death, not "the Jews."

I have tried to "say" all of this in sculpture. Pilate washes his hands and seems to appeal to Jesus to convict himself. Jesus stands defiantly, hands tied, wearily denying all that Pilate is saying and all that Pilot's world of violence and fear demands.

3. Carter, *Matthew and Empire*, 161.

Not Your World

Part Three

Jesus' Wisdom in Daily Life: Introduction

Part Three deals with issues that confront us in our daily lives. We need the best wisdom available when we make decisions for or against something. For example, when we have to choose how to earn, spend, or save money, or how to deal with taxes or with shame, or how to resist temptation, where do we go for help and guidance? We need wisdom to guide us to the best decisions. As Christians who claim to follow Jesus, we can ask a simple question, "What would Jesus do?" and then just do that. But how do we know what Jesus would do in our situation or even what exactly he did do in his own situation, given the disagreements between the different gospel reports? How do we span two thousand years and vastly different contexts?

Part Three takes specific issues and seeks answers to these questions by recognizing these great differences, employing the prism of biblical scholarship, and by including the political and economic contexts of Jesus' time and our own. I will continue to include visual images as done in Parts 1 and 2.

27

Wealth

"It is easier for a camel to go through the eye of a needle than for someone who is rich to enter the Kingdom of God."

(Mark 10:23–27; also Luke 18:18–25)

Then Jesus looked around and said to his disciples, "How hard it will be for those who have wealth to enter the kingdom of God!" And the disciples were perplexed at these words. But Jesus said to them again, "Children, how hard it is to enter the kingdom of God! It is easier for a camel to go through the eye of a needle than for someone who is rich to enter the kingdom of God." They were greatly astounded and said to one another, "Then who can be saved?" Jesus looked at them and said, "For mortals it is impossible, but not for God; for God all things are possible."

Why is it so hard for a rich man (or woman) to enter God's Empire? Buckminster Fuller is often quoted as saying that people wear blinders and they seldom see beyond their feedbags—meaning that our vision is almost always limited by our daily economic situation. What puts bread on our table determines our general perspective on life.

I made a series of three presentations of an early version of this book and DVD to a very prosperous church in a highly affluent New York suburb. I explained the need to avoid false assumptions such as that people in Jesus' audiences were middle class, although most of the folks in this particular church were way above middle class economically. I pointed out how Jesus' audience was "harassed and helpless" (Matt 9:36) because Rome extorted enormous taxes, tributes, and rents, leaving them destitute, and that their revolts against Rome were crushed mercilessly. One of the church's lay leaders questioned my analysis early in the first session and said that *I* was making a false assumption by claiming that Jesus' peasant audience was so poor, miserable, and eager to resist Roman domination. He went on to declare that the Jews were much better off under the Roman occupation. Well, I had expected some questioning and was ready for it, although I was a bit shocked by the claim that the Jews were better off. But I "girded my loins" for a quick, powerful, factual, and visual response.

The context of this wisdom saying is of the rich man who follows all the wisdom he knows but is not satisfied that he will be welcome in God's Empire. He would not sell all he had and give it to the poor in order to enter God's Empire. So Jesus gave this comical proverb about a camel going through a needle's eye.

This sculpture has images of a former chief economic advisor to a President and a Secretary of the Treasury in the USA trying to push and pull a big camel through a small needle's eye. The fearful camel and top-hatted and tuxedoed rich men, whose efforts are, of course, hopeless, envision the absurdity of Jesus' image. For God's Empire cannot be bought. It can only be given freely by grace, which grace empowers the generous sharing of wealth and just economic structures, structures that are not "too big to fail." For Jesus' wisdom applies to our time as well as his own and applies to individuals as well as corporate economic systems.

Eye of a Needle

I was eager, perhaps too eager, to point out to my affluent New York questioner that against hopeless odds the Jews rebelled against their foreign occupiers four different times in Jesus' period. Two were before Jesus grew up and two after Rome killed him. (The Maccabean revolt in 160 BCE against the Greek/Seleucid Empire, against Rome in 4 CE, again in 66–70 CE and another in 132–135 CE.) Then I summed up: "With all these suicidal revolts, the Jews must not have been very pleased with their occupying enemies."

I realized later in a cooler moment that my questioner was right about one thing: We cannot avoid our social location.[1] We all always see things through our own context, especially our economic context (our feedbags). But we can try to acknowledge it and allow for our limited vision. I was sad that my questioner did not return to any more of these sessions that I was leading, although he was present at church those Sundays. And I am confident that, like me, he did not sell all he had and give it to the poor.

1. See Segovia and Tolbert, *Reading from this Place*.

28

Taxes

"Give to the emperor the things that are the emperor's,
and to God the things that are God's."

(Mark 12:13–17; also Matt 22:15–22;
Luke 20:20–26; Ps 24:1; 95:4–5)

Then they sent to him some Pharisees and some Herodians to trap him in what he said. And they came and said to him, "Teacher, we know that you are sincere, and show deference to no one; for you do not regard people with partiality, but teach the way of God in accordance with truth. Is it lawful to pay taxes to the emperor, or not? Should we pay them, or should we not?" But knowing their hypocrisy, he said to them, "Why are you putting me to the test? Bring me a denarius and let me see it." And they brought one. Then he said to them, "Whose head is this, and whose title?" They answered, "The emperor's." Jesus said to them, "Give to the emperor the things that are the emperor's, and to God the things that are God's."

THIS PROVERB IS A good example of hidden discourse, for Jesus says one thing on one level and a different thing on another level. The Pharisees and Herodians are setting a trap for him. So he says two things in this one response concerning to whom they owe taxes. The first level says nothing because he simply says pay to Caesar and to God what they are each due. This gets him out of the trap, but he does not say what things are Caesar's or what things are God's. On a second level that Jews would understand, everything is God's and Caesar is due only what God grants him, if anything. The Romans would not recognize this scriptural wisdom.

We experience such hidden discourse often. When I was a teen trying to play football, my coach commented on my effort with, "On a scale of one to ten, you are doing the best you can." On one level his words seemed to be a compliment. On another level they said nothing.

We find another example of saying two things on two different levels in a famous story of a rabbi in the middle ages who had a false reputation for teaching animals how to talk. The prince came to him demanding that the rabbi teach his dog to talk. The rabbi agreed, hoping to appease the prince. His wife said he was crazy to agree because she knew he could not teach a dog to talk. But he responded to her that he had a whole year to deal with his promise. When the prince came for his "talking" dog the next year, the rabbi was ready.

But first more on this scripture passage.

This proverb is clearly both private and public wisdom, for individuals pay taxes but the state (the public) takes them for various just and unjust purposes. However, this saying is often taken to legitimize two realms of responsibility (Luther's two kingdoms) that have no connection to each other and to grant to the state (the emperor) the taxes he demands. Such an interpretation ignores the wisdom of Jesus' own Bible. The First Testament is clear that all creation belongs to God (Psalm 24, "The Earth is the Lord's" and Psalm 95:4–5, "In his hand are the depths of the earth; the heights of the mountains are his also. The sea is his for he made it, and the dry land, which his hands have formed.").

The Roman Empire is not some realm set apart from God's earth. When Jesus is asked about paying taxes to the emperor, Jesus, sensing a trap, asks for a coin and inquires whose image is on it. We can infer from his asking for a coin that Jesus did not carry a coin and that when his would-be entrappers provided one, they thereby admitted to carrying the emperor's image—forbidden for Jews at that time. When they show the emperor's image, Jesus answered their question on one level without saying anything. He said to give the emperor the things that are his and to God what is God's. But on a second level that the Jews would understand Jesus here is saying, we should give God everything, including taxes, because God owns everything—which leaves nothing for the emperor, unless it is granted him by God.

In these sculptures I have tried to show the wisdom of this saying in a two sided relief in the shape of a coin. On the first side the emperor points to himself with his left hand and holds up a round shape of emptiness with his right. On the second side, Jesus gestures that all creation is God's; and it is to God, who owns all creation, that we owe all, including our taxes.

What is Caesar's.

What is God's

When the prince returned the next year to retrieve his "talking" dog, the rabbi said the dog talked very well and had told him everything that went on in the prince's court. The dog even told him how the prince often frequented the local brothel. The prince was livid at this gossip and asked where the dog was so he could kill it. The rabbi replied, "Not to worry, I have taken care of that too." The "weapons of the weak" include saying things in a hidden discourse.

29

Accepting New Ideas

"No one puts new wine in old wineskins."

(Mark 2:22; also Matt 9:17; Luke 5:36)

"No one puts new wine into old wineskins; otherwise, the wine will burst the skins, and the wine is lost, and so are the skins; but one puts new wine into fresh wineskins."

THE COMMON UNDERSTANDING OF this saying is that it is personal advice to individuals not to linger in the past but to move on to new ways, not to be held back by old, rigid ideas, which, like old, dried out wineskins, break when new wine is poured into them. The fermenting gases of new wine expand and break open the old skin.

However, I imagined this saying to have more than individual application and recognizied that in Jesus' time the dominant economic and political power of Rome controlled all of its colonies including Gallilee, Samaria, and Judea. They did this by extracting their resources to pay for its governance and wars and to keep the tiny fraction of the wealthy living in luxury. This was enforced with extortionist taxes, tributes, and rents, the non-payment of which was considered sedition. The Roman army would make sure payments were made. Also, in Judea the high priests were appointed by Rome to keep this system functioning. They and other temple elites who enjoyed the wealth which came from enforcing their assigned task, controlled the economic and political structure. That was the old wine skin structure.

This saying of Jesus suggests that the whole structure and assumptions of oppression must be changed, not just the private behavior of individuals. Postcolonial scholar, Musa Dube, quoted earlier in this book, vividly illustrated this old wine skin thinking when she went from her home in Botswana in the huge continent of Africa to the small island called "Great Britain." She wondered why this little island was called "*Great*" Britain or why it was said that "the sun never sets on it" when she rarely saw the sun in London. Then she analyzed how the passage in John 4:1–42 was used by western missionaries to justify the domestication of non-western people who are viewed as a "field ripe for harvesting" (John 4:35). People are not fields to enter and reap or domesticate. That is old wine skin thinking.[1] We must have new wine skin thinking that includes non-western perspectives, including those of Africa.

In this image, with his left hand Jesus is rejecting the temple, its guards, as well as the image of the emperor. With his right hand he is affirming the poor child.

By contrast, the high priest is pointing to the temple and the emperor to whom the old wisdom calls us to pay homage. With his left hand he is rejecting the child and Jesus' way of honoring " the little ones" (Matt 18:6). In the center of the image is a jar of new wine being poured into the old wineskin. That old skin explodes suggesting what happens to new ways of ordering the world according to God's purposes. It will explode when it is "poured" into the old, existing structures of the oppressive Roman economic and political system.

Jesus' saying suggests that we move beyond our own narrow vision of economic self-interest, nationalism, homophobia, and myopia to new wine skins thinking that is receptive to new ideas. New wine in new wine skins takes time to age, but like an open and affirming vision that accepts new ideas, the new wine in new skins makes for the best and most lasting nourishment.

1. In Surgirtharajah, *The Postcolonial Bible*, 120.

Old and New Wine

30

Defilement/Shame

"Nothing outside a person . . . by going in can defile."

(Mark 7:14–23; also Gos. Thom. 14)

Then he called the crowd again and said to them, "Listen to me, all of you, and understand: there is nothing outside a person that by going in can defile, but the things that come out are what defile."

WHY DO THINGS THAT come out of us defile us? According to scholars, Mark probably added this explanation:

> When he had left the crowd and entered the house, his disciples asked him about the parable. He said to them, "Then do you also fail to understand? Do you not see that whatever goes into a person from the outside cannot defile since it enters, not the heart but the stomach, and goes out into the sewer?" (Thus he declared all foods clean.) And he said, "It is what comes out of a person that defiles. For it is from within, from the human heart, that evil intentions come: fornication, theft, murder, adultery, avarice, wickedness, deceit, licentiousness, envy slander, pride, folly. All these evil things come from within, and they defile a person."

Scholars tell us that while the main wisdom saying, no doubt, comes from Jesus, the explanation of its meaning is probably added by Mark to deal with issues in Mark's time, around 70 CE. The long list of "wicked intentions" is a later and commonly cited list of evils. So what is most critical is that the main saying reverses the ancient holiness codes and dietary rules that restrict what people take in from the outside. It is what we put out that matters and can defile us rather than what we take in.

Jesus' saying is not limited to food and what goes into or comes out of our stomachs; it focuses on what comes out of our hearts, our decisions, and actions. He was not a nutritionist. Nor were people in his time made obese by fast food or excited by media pornography or seduced by modern ideologies that we take in. In Jesus' time, it was not a few integrated agricultural conglomerates and corporate monopolies who controlled the food supply. Nor was the media saturated with talk show ideologues or lewd images as it is today.

In any case, Jesus was concerned with what comes out of us. That is what can defile, corrupt, and shame us. (There are other words than "defile" and "shame" that capture this blame-the-victim tactic: "stain", "soil", "make unworthy", "unclean," and "slime.") Jesus rejects the outside rules that tell us to "tithe mint, dill and cummin", and he affirms "the weightier matters of the law: justice and mercy and faith" (Matt 23:23).

To be sure, living in our time demands careful intake of food as well as images and ideas. But Jesus was stressing the defilement of our active behavior, not our passive consumption. We defile ourselves when we hurt, diminish, and destroy ourselves, other people, and God's creation.

A striking case of what goes into our bodies happens with rape, kidnapping, or the much lesser violation of robbery. A rape, kidnapping, or robbery victim often feels defiled, shamed, corrupted, unclean, stained, soiled, unworthy, or slimed. We and others who are assaulted often blame ourselves instead of the aggressor. But Jesus' wisdom is that it is the rapists, kidnappers, and robbers who are the defiled and shamed persons because of their active, invading behavior, not the passive victim of the attack. What a miraculous blessing it is when victims understand deeply that they are not blamed or condemned for what is done to them. There is no shame in being abused. The defilement is only on the abuser who is held accountable for that outer behavior.

Defiling and shaming others is also a political tool that is very effective because it puts the domination (colonization) inside the dominated, colonized person(s). So then they limit themselves to obeying unjust rules and accepting the domination as something they "deserve" because they see themselves as already defiled, shamed, and unworthy. I will consider this important concept more, later. For now I want to illustrate this wisdom saying with a personal experience.

Some years ago I was experiencing great stress. I was paying tuition for the schooling of my three children, rebuilding an old farm, and commuting to New York when I was not on the road to speaking commitments all over the country. Then I lost my job. I felt defeated and, at my lowest, defiled and shamed. I had to support my family but I had no job. I internalized the negative judgment I thought others had of me. "Unemployed" felt like my shameful title.

Blessedly, I had an outlet for my stress. Besides job-hunting, I increased my work in art. One of the pieces I sketched and sculpted was a workhorse pulling an immovable wagon of rocks. He was straining every muscle, struggling with all his might to pull this "Heavy Burden," the name I gave this clay relief sculpture. But it was too much for him. That was how I felt then. As with the workhorse, my own burdens were overwhelming me.

Heavy Burden

The stress in my life was way beyond my capacity to handle. But I kept up the drawing and sculpting and carved the overwhelmed workhorse in wood. Only much later did I consciously connect this workhorse's struggle with my own burdens. This wooden workhorse was still straining all he could, but I realized then that the heavy burden of the cart of rocks was not there.

No Shame

So it was with me. The stress and shame (defilement) was all on the outside. I had chosen to internalize it. That shame did not exist in reality. Only in my moments of self-loathing did it exist, and only in my negative imagination. The heavy burden was absent though it occasionally returned to my view of myself at low points when I nursed it back to life. I began to sculpt other horses in clay and wood but without the heavy burden and without the strained muscles and stressful posture. Those horses were free to run, even to prance.

Running Free

The impossible load was gone, and if I could fully realize this for myself, I would be truly blessed. I was not defiled by outside forces and would only be defiled (shamed, corrupted, unclean, stained, soiled, unworthy, slimed) if I had really acted out my stress by harming myself or someone else. I was blessed to have the gift of art as a better outlet than attacking myself or others. Eight months after I lost my job, I found another job I really liked.

31

Down Time

"The sabbath was made for humankind. . . ."

"The sabbath was made for humankind, and not humankind for the sabbath; so the Son of Man is Lord even of the sabbath."

(Mark 2:27; also Matt 12:1–8; Luke 6:1–5)

I ASK MYSELF, "WHEN was the last time you took a break to center yourself and calm down enough from your frantic schedule to take stock of where you are going and why?" It is so easy to keep going 24/7. "I've got to compete. That's how one wins," I rationalize.

The need to pause to get our bearings is what the sabbath rest is about, and our religious tradition calls us to take stock at least every seven days. There is no magic in the number seven, but wisdom tells us that if we do not slow down at least once a week, we can easily get overwhelmed or underwhelmed and start acting funny.

A friend of mine was working about eighty hours a week trying to "get ahead," as he put it. He did not take days off or vacations or spend much time with his spouse. He might have been called a workaholic. There is a modern saying for this obsession: "He has a monkey on his back." But he loved his work, mostly on a computer, and stayed at it day and night because it made him feel powerful, in charge, and proud that he could provide for his family. He figured this was what life was all about and expected his spouse to appreciate it too. One day she got him to take off a few hours to meet him at a nice building where he had never been. It was an office building where her attorney handed him divorce papers. She left him cold.

He had been overwhelmed with work. He had made profit and success in the business world his god, and the way to succeed was to work very hard. But Jesus' wisdom for today might well be translated, "Work is made for humanity, not humanity for work." My friend needed a sabbath rest. When his spouse left him, he was lost. His spirit was gone. He was overwhelmed with depression. His proud self-assurance turned to self-loathing because he condemned himself for his failure. He did not take time for a sabbath rest, renewal, and priority setting.

However, rigidly keeping the sabbath can also be detrimental. The sabbath itself can become a burden that keeps us anxious and task-oriented, defeating the purpose of sabbath itself. Jesus' wisdom turns this rigidity around and says that the sabbath was meant to assure our health and not to burden us with unhealthy do's and don't' s. It is wise to rest, and while you are at it, to realize that you are not the center of the universe as my friend seemed to think he was. But neither was he a miserable, unworthy person as he came to feel when his world crashed. No, God is the center and you/we are already worthy and beloved children of God.

All three synoptic gospels have a version of this saying although Matthew and Luke dropped the first half of Mark's version about the sabbath being made for humanity. They dropped that and kept the second part that the Son of Man (meaning either Jesus or all humanity) is Lord of the sabbath. Just as Genesis 1:26 gives Adam and Eve (humanity) dominion over the creatures, so Jesus extended that dominion over the sabbath. Human welfare comes first, before the rules and laws that we invent.

But religion in Jesus' time (and our own) got caught up in the social, economic, and political system, which turns the intent of wisdom inside out and upside down. Instead of rest and renewal (the goal of Sabbath), the sabbath becomes one more burden to weigh us down, or it is used to keep others in line. The rules for keeping the sabbath became so strict in Jesus' time that the leaders even condemned Jesus for healing people on the sabbath (Matt 12:9–14; Luke 6:7–10; 14:2–6; John 5:2–18).

My friend sought the goal of success in society that values profit above all else and rewards extreme work schedules that increase that profit. The more work, the better. But work easily becomes an end in itself rather than a means to a whole and healthy life.

This profit motive is not just a matter of private morality. My friend's company that set the values by which he lived spoke a different language from common decency. As R. S. Sugirtharajah points out: "the language of guilt, truth and responsibility are foreign to present-day multinational capitalists, international power brokers, transnational bankers and military strategists. They speak a different language—the language of success, efficiency, performance and profit."[1]

In Jesus' time and in our own time religious leaders are caught up in maintaining corrupt social systems that, on the one hand, judge, condemn, and tax people way beyond their capacity. So people turn that judgment in on themselves as self-loathing and frantically keep running faster on the work treadmill. On the other hand, the very few who benefit from the system are easily tempted to see themselves as "Lords of the Universe," as my friend seemed to do before he got this wake-up call from his wife.

Jesus confronted this small group who gamed the system—that is, the leaders who were both political and religious authorities (they were one and the same)—for their hypocrisy and called for the sabbath to be returned to a time of rest and renewal. In our time we are also called by Jesus to get the monkey off our backs, to get off the treadmill (the fast track, the fast lane, the workaholism) and to reset our priorities, where we are going and why. We can stop trying to prove we are worthy of the success standards of our social system and realize that we are already worthy and need to prove nothing. Instead of having no time to take it easy, we are called by Jesus' wisdom to grab some down time and reset our direction so that we can love others, smell the flowers, and praise the Creator who makes them bloom. We have it in our power to send the monkeys on our backs off to the jungle.

No Back Monkeys

1. Sugirtharajah, *The Postcolonial Bible*, 112.

32

Introducing Addictions as Modern Demons

"A kingdom divided against itself, that kingdom cannot stand."

(Mark 3:20–27; Matt 12:22–32;
Luke 11:14; Gos. Thom. 35:1–2)

And the crowd came together again, so that they could not even eat. When his family heard it, they went out to restrain him, for people were saying, "He has gone out of his mind." And the scribes who came down from Jerusalem said, "He has Beelzebul, and by the ruler of the demons he casts out demons." And he called them to him, and spoke to them in parables, "How can Satan cast out Satan? If a kingdom is divided against itself, that kingdom cannot stand. And if a house is divided against itself, that house will not be able to stand. And if Satan has risen up against himself and is divided, he cannot stand, but his end has come. But no one can enter a strong man's house and plunder his property without first tying up the strong man; then indeed the house can be plundered."

I TOOK A BREAK from working on this saying to mow a pasture behind my house and passed a birdhouse that I had recently nailed to a tree for blue birds to nest in. The birdhouse was old but I was still surprised that it had fallen down in pieces. Why had it fallen apart so soon?

That afternoon I asked a neighbor, Hannah Suthers, who is a biologist and avid ornithologist. She explained the destroyed birdhouse this way: "A Great Breasted Flycatcher is a cavity nester who wanted the bird house. But some sparrows wanted the house for their nest too. I watched them fight viciously over who owned the house and it fell as a result."

It was literally a divided house that was so destroyed that no birds could use it, not the Great Breasted Flycatcher, not the Sparrows, and certainly not the Blue Birds. I thought: what an apt application of this saying! This divided house could not stand and everybody suffers. So I went back to work on this piece of Jesus' wisdom with this divided birdhouse in mind.

This saying has often been used as a call to unity for "division in the ranks" can lead to defeat. Ben Franklin is often quoted as saying to other rebelling patriots, "We must hang together or surely we will hang separately." His words call for political unity. But Jesus' saying also deals with individual and family unity, for a "house" often means a "family" that must stick together to succeed or survive. Even an individual person who is not "together," who is divided, suggests that he or she has a mental problem that in Jesus' time is called an unclean spirit or demon. This saying is in the context of demon possession and exorcisms of demons, concepts that are often strange to people today. Furthermore, the passage says that Jesus himself was thought to have "gone out of his mind so that his family went out to restrain him" (v. 21). That is, they tried what we might call a "family intervention," because they thought Jesus had an unclean spirit or demon. They thought he was acting crazy. So individuals, families, as well as entire nations can be divided and can therefore fall. Or, as people thought and spoke in ancient times, all can have a "demon." We will distinguish here private persons (individuals and families) from public groups of people (whole nations or societies) who can be divided.

Yet, Jesus turned around this accusation of himself having a demon. (In the sculpture below, note Jesus' family on the left pulling him back home even though that home is divided and falling apart.) Then the lawyers showed up from downtown and heaped even more charges on him. (Note the figures on the right that Jesus [back turned] ignores while casting out the demon of the divided mad man in the center.) They claimed that Jesus was exorcizing demons in the name of the top demon named Beelzebul or Satan.

Private Demons

How do we translate "demons" and "exorcism of demons" into our time when only a few people believe demons even exist and some who do, misuse that belief to condemn traits in people of which they disapprove? An example is a "homosexual demon" which some Bible literalists try to exorcize. Ancient people personified spiritual beings such as evil=Satan or Love=God. We in our time have these same experiences but usually do not personify them. That is, we know some behavior is disapproved of by some people, but we rarely speak of the one disapproved of as Satan or a demon. This is true except for people who take the Bible literally. Then serious problems arise, such as trying to exorcize a "homosexual demon"[1] —or for that matter a "homophobic demon." Literalism can be very dangerous.

One way to translate demons into modern usage is to list some of the "-isms" that haunt people today: alcoholism, terrorism, communism, racism, capitalism, nationalism, militarism, consumerism, socialism, etc. Of course, adding the suffix "-ism" does not necessarily make

1. See Joseph Laycock, "Modern Exorcism: Trading Autonomy for Demonology", *Sightings*, 7/8/10, c/o ktobey@chicago.edu where belief in demons and exorcism is said to be on the rise, but is now called "Deliverance Ministries."

something a demon or evil. But when we are blinded by or obsessed by an "-ism" so that we hurt ourselves or others, we may be possessed by it. In Jesus' time people would have said we had an unclean spirit or demon that needed to be removed, cast out, or exorcized. That was how first-century people named what is now called an obsession or an addiction.

There are many levels of addictions. Mark mentioned first the divided empire, then the divided house that could not stand. The public (empire) and the private (house) are mixed together in the Bible. In order to sort this out I will distinguish these two areas. The following chapter is about private addictions, and the subsequent one about public addictions.

33

Private Addictions

WHAT ARE SOME SPECIFIC demons (addictions) that blind and hurt others and ourselves? One example on a personal level is a problem a friend of mine suffers. He seems possessed with the failure of his business many years ago during an economic downturn in which he had to declare bankruptcy. Now he barely gets out of bed but instead spends his days going over his trauma of long ago. He says he is a terrible person and wonders why he should go on living. This demon or addiction to business success/failure blinds him to the God-given blessing of affirmation and puts him on the road to self-destruction. His inner house is divided, perhaps beyond repair.

Psychological counseling can help my friend, who is so depressed he stays in bed—if he will cooperate with it. Counselors are trained to see and name our addictions or demons, and can help us see that to which we are blind. They help us to reunite our divided selves and so serve as something like exorcists did in biblical times.

The most persistent and hard-to-treat private addiction is substance abuse which includes alcoholism and drug abuse. Psychological counseling is only a start in a long process of ridding people of this demon. The twelve-step program of Alcoholics Anonymous has proved the most effective *if* the addict sticks with it and determines to make it work.

The divided houses of our personal and public lives must find the courage to face and cast out our addictions, our demons or, like the birds in my pasture, we will destroy our houses so no one can live in them.

34

Public Addictions

"Come out of the man you unclean spirit."

(Mark 5:1–13; Matt 8:28–34; Luke 8:26–39)

They came to the other side of the lake, to the country of the Gerasenes. And when he had stepped out of the boat, immediately a man out of the tombs with an unclean spirit met him. He lived among the tombs; and no one could restrain him anymore, even with a chain; for he had often been restrained with shackles and chains, but the chains he wrenched apart, and the shackles he broke in pieces; and no one had the strength to subdue him. Night and day among the tombs and on the mountains he was always howling and bruising himself with stones. When he saw Jesus from a distance, he ran and bowed down before him; and he shouted at the top of his voice, "What have you to do with me, Jesus, Son of the Most High God? I adjure you by God, do not torment me." For he had said to him, "Come out of the man, you unclean spirit!" Then Jesus asked him, "What is your name?" He replied, "My name is Legion; for we are many." He begged him earnestly not to send them out of the country. Now there on the hillside a great herd of swine was feeding; and the unclean spirits begged him, "Send us into the swine; let us enter them." So he gave them permission. And the unclean spirits came out and entered the swine; and the herd, numbering about two thousand, rushed down the steep bank into the sea, and were drowned in the sea.

As for public addictions, we have a vivid example in the Gospel of Mark. Mark reports two chapters later (5:1–13) that Jesus cast out a demon called "Legion." A legion is the name of a corps of 6,000 Roman soldiers. Jesus sent the demon Legion into pigs that drowned in the sea. Some New Testament scholars spell out the meaning of this demon called "Legion." For example, Warren Carter says,

> Mark shows Rome's empire to be of the devil in the story of the man possessed by a demon (Mark 5:1–20) . . . .The demon begs Jesus not to send it out of the country that they occupy (5:10). Instead, Jesus casts it into a herd of pigs that destroys itself in the sea (5:13). Significantly, the mascot of Rome's tenth Fretensis legion that destroyed Jerusalem in 70 (about the time Mark was written) was the pig."[1]

That pig was probably a wild boar which is *fretensis* or ferocious.

Public addictions/demons in our time are less obvious but certainly very deadly. For instance, we see how the demon of white supremacy/racism has divided our national house with the terrible results of slavery, the Civil War, and segregation. On a global scale, colonialism of white people once dominated most of the earth's people of color. It still persists in what is called "neo colonialism." This addiction to white supremacy must be completely exorcized because it destroys our public houses. A number of white political figures in our time express the hope that our first African American president will fail at any cost, even if it brings suffering down on all of us. This is so blindingly irrational as to suggest it is another case of addiction to white supremacy.

In this sculpture the mad man on the left is breaking his chains and screaming. Jesus in the center is casting out the demon Legion as Caesar (upper left) falls from his pedestal and Roman legions turn into pigs who fall into the sea on the far right.

1. Carter, *The Roman Empire and the New Testament*, 17.

Public Demons

Our national leaders of both parties in the U.S. declare that we are addicted to oil, and we see each day how destructive it is to our nation and the natural world. Yet, like an addict, we cannot seem to move beyond it; we are blind to that addiction even though it hurts us, others, and nature.

On a public level I believe it is the role of honest politicians, artists, and religious leaders to name and unmask our addictions to social ills such as addiction to white supremacy and fossil fuels, although this may come as a new job description to many.

We return to Mark 3:27 and the image of the "strongman," which Mark probably added to the divided empire and house. This is clearly a public rather than private demon/addiction. There is much debate among scholars about the meaning of Jesus' saying about the strongman who must be tied up before his property can be plundered. No one knows its meaning for certain, but it is not far-fetched to claim that the "strongman" refers to Rome, for Jesus' audience experienced the brutal strength of the Roman power every day. Who else in their experience would merit the "strongman" name besides Rome or Caesar or Pilate? What is certain is that only an indivisible counterforce could prevail against the highly organized Roman military. But such a force would have to resist on terms other than military might. For Rome was too strong for that. The force would have to be a highly united nonviolent resistance force that was immune to division in the ranks. This was what Jesus tried to teach: aggressive resistance that was nonviolent. Gandhi and King, among others, proved the success of such nonviolent resistance in modern times.

35

Speaking Up

"Is a lamp . . . put under a bushel basket?"
(Mark 4:21–22; also Luke 8:16; 11:33; Matt 5:15; Gos. Thom. 33)

"Is a lamp brought in to be put under the bushel basket, or under the bed, and not on the lamp stand? For there is nothing hidden except to be disclosed, nor any secret except to come to light."

THIS SAYING OCCURS IN Mark, Matthew, Thomas, and twice in Luke. Scholars declare it came from Jesus but the gospel writers placed it in different contexts. It probably was a free-floating saying that the evangelists attached to their varying contexts in each gospel. It is helpful to look at what passages precede this saying in each gospel to determine that context. Mark and the first of Luke's sayings (8:16) are preceded by the interpretation of the Sower parable in which those who hear and accept Jesus' message are like seeds in rich soil that grow and produce fruit thirty, sixty, and a hundred fold. This saying in Matthew follows the Beatitudes and the declaration that the disciples are the salt of the earth. Thomas places the saying after two other statements that a prophet is not welcome in his own home and the lamp cannot be hidden any more than a city on a hill can be hidden. The second Luke placement of the saying (11:33) follows an apocalyptic judgment day warning.

These various contexts of the saying about not hiding a lamp are important because they clarify what the metaphors of the lamp, salt, seed, or city on a hill refer to that should not be hidden. What do these metaphors stand for? For many Christians they stand for the personal Good News that each of us is individually loved, affirmed, and justified by freely given grace that we accept on faith. This can hardly be questioned as a traditional and an altogether appropriate interpretation of its meaning. Yet in addition to this private blessing of God's love, that lamp can also mean a public gift of peace and justice. That is what the Beatitudes are all about: hope for the poor, the mourners, the gentle, and hungry, and merciful, the pure in heart, and peacemakers, and the persecuted. These are not only private hopes but also public hopes and promises. They are the lamp we must not hide. The lamp is both a private gift of God's forgiving love and a public gift of shalom for all these groups of the poor, hungry, and persecuted people.

This context in which Matthew sets the saying about the lamp can mean the same individual and public peace and justice in Mark and Luke 8:16 if we understand that the Sower's seed or word is this same Good News that lands on fertile ground and produces abundant fruit. Jesus' message (lamp, seed, salt, city on a hill) is compared to the political and economic suffering of the people to whom Jesus was speaking. Jesus' audience was the poor, the hungry, and the persecuted ones who lived in a Roman-occupied colony ruled by violence, fear, torture and daily humiliation. That was the Empire of Rome. Compared to that Roman Empire, Jesus presented the Empire of God that was the exact opposite, and it, like a lamp, must not be hidden. That message was the seed, salt, lamp, and city on a hill of nonviolence, courage and dignity. That is the message that must not be hidden by silence, confusion, denial, or any other form of opposition to God's loving Empire.

How do we hide this message? Usually by silence.

When Martin Luther King, Jr. was leading the Civil Rights movement, other clergy warned him to back off, to be silent, not to cause a stink. In particular, there was the demonstration in Birmingham, Alabama that other clergy said was "unwise and untimely." King responded with his famous, "Letter from a Birmingham Jail."[1] In it he said that the church so often is "an archdefender of the status quo. Far from being disturbed by the presence of the church, the power structure of the average community is consoled by the church's silence. . . ." King actually expected that he would be supported by religious leaders but, "[i]

1. *Christian Century*, 767–73.

nstead, some have been outright opponents, refusing to understand the freedom movement and misrepresenting its leaders; all too many others have been more cautious than courageous and have remained silent and secure behind stained glass windows."[2]

It was the good church people who so disappointed him by their silence for they hid the lamp of God's love under a basket. King said, "We will have to repent in this generation not merely for the hateful words and actions of bad people but for the appalling silence of the good people."[3]

King did recognize the support he got from a few "noble souls from the ranks of organized religion calling them the "spiritual salt." He said, "they have acted in the faith that right defeated is stronger than evil triumphant. Their witness has been the spiritual salt that has preserved the true meaning of the gospel in these troubled times."[4]

Don't Hide Your Light

This strength of love was firm in his life as he faced the powerful forces that had all of the power and might of the government, media, and even the white church. But he said in another writing, "In a world

2. Ibid., 772.
3. Ibid., 779.
4. Ibid., 772–73.

depending on force, coercive tyranny, bloody violence, you are challenged to follow the way of love. You will discover that unarmed love is the most powerful force in all the world."[5]

In this sculpture, King is writing that letter behind the bars of the Birmingham jail. In the background lurks the KKK, and the lynching of a black man hangs in his mind. On the left, two clergymen advise silence from the church.

Of course, on some occasions it is wise to be silent. Jesus himself was silent before Pilate. But silence is supreme cowardice in many cases. Jesus was clear about not hiding his message under a basket. So too we must speak out against violence, fear, torture, and humiliation of all people by all empires, even an empire as strong as Rome. King, reflecting Jesus' words, proclaimed that love is truly stronger than evil and stronger than the silence that enables evil to thrive when love is hidden under a basket. That is the lamp, salt, seed, city on a hill, the metaphors Jesus used for the love, peace, and justice of God that cannot be hidden. It will be "disclosed" and "come to light."

5. King, *Strength to Love*, 255–6.

36

Dealing with Kinfolks

"Whoever does the will of God is my brother and sister and mother."

(Mark 3:34–36; also Matt 12:46–50;
Luke 8:19–28; *Gos. Thom.* 99)

Then his mother and his brothers came; and standing outside, they sent to him and called him. A crowd was sitting around him; and they said to him, "Your mother and your brothers and sisters are outside, asking for you." And he replied, "Who are my mother and my brothers?" And looking at those who sat around him, he said, "Here are my mother and my brothers! Whoever does the will of God is my brother and sister and mother."

THIS SAYING IS ONE of the "hard sayings" for us in the twenty-first century because the rules of family life that in ancient times were dominated by the father have changed so much. In Jesus' time patriarchy ruled, families were large, and the father was expected to control his wife (or wives), sons, daughters, and other relatives, servants, and all living in "his" house.

Who Are My Kin?

Families made up clans and tribes, and so fathers were also accountable to the larger tribal, village, and religious leaders. By Jesus' time these leaders were themselves accountable to their Roman rulers who demanded that they keep the (Roman) peace. At the top of this hierarchy was the emperor who was called not only "father" (*pater*) but also "Father of the Fatherland" (*pater patriae*). "This title not only combined religion and politics, but it also depicted the empire as a large household over which the emperor, like a household's father, exercised authority and protection in return for obedience and submissive devotion."[1]

So when Jesus began to challenge these authorities, his actions were so radical and so dangerous that he was considered "out of his mind;" and his family sought to restrain him (Mark 3:21). We know from Mark 6:3 and Matt 13:55 that Jesus had four brothers: James, Jose, Simon, and Judas, as well as unnamed sisters.[2]

Although his hometown folk in Nazareth were astounded at his wisdom (Mark 6:2), they also "took offense at him" (Mark 6:3b). Jesus responded to this offense by saying, "Prophets are not without honor, except in their hometown and among their own kin, and in their own

1. Carter, *The Roman Empire and the New Testament*, 32.

2. True to the rules of patriarchy, his sisters' names are not mentioned in the gospels.

house" (Mark 6:4). When Jesus' family came asking for him later while he was teaching, Jesus replied, "Who are my mother and brothers? And looking at those who sat around him, he said, "Here are my mother and my brothers! Whoever does the will of God is my brother and sister and mother" (Mark 3:34–35).

By challenging his blood relatives and thus the patriarchal system, Jesus was subverting the whole structure that held this society together. If only those who do the will of God are his brother, sisters, and mother, then he is calling for a radical change in the expectations of accountability. No longer would people answer only to their fathers, tribal, village leaders, and their Roman overlords. Instead, they would answer only to God. No wonder his family wanted to restrain him. And no wonder the people were astonished and took offense. He was being a traitor to the social structure and the conventional wisdom. Soon after, Mark's Jesus will predict that he will be "rejected by the elders, the chief priests and the scribes, and be killed" (Mark 8:31).

Although Jesus' earthly father, Joseph, is oddly absent in the gospels after Jesus' youth, his brothers fill in for him and try to keep Jesus from destroying the whole paternalistic structure and getting killed for it. Yet, Jesus persists in his challenges of this system and refuses to honor the authorities all the way up the hierarchy to Caesar. He insists that they "Call no one your father on earth, for you have one Father—the one in heaven" (Matt 23:9).

It is no overstatement to conclude from this saying about kinship that is based on who does the will of God that it was a challenge to the whole Roman Empire. For by undercutting patriarchy Jesus struck at the foundation of the whole system. Warren Carter gives a good summary in his book on Matthew of how Jesus subverts

> imperial claims and creates an alternative empire and way of life . . . an empire that prefers egalitarian structures rather than Rome's hierarchy (23:8–12; chs. 19–20), an empire that emphasizes service not Rome's domination (20:24–28), that values inclusion not the elites' exclusion (9:9–13), mutuality not patriarchy (19:3–9; 23:9) . . . inclusive love not privilege (5:45), mercy not intimidating violence (9:13; 26:52,) God not Caesar (22:15–22).[3]

This is the public interpretation of this wisdom saying of Jesus. What about private, family life? Today, we too are challenged to seek an

3. Carter, *Matthew and Empire*, 61. The references are in Matthew.

alternative way of life, to serve and include others, to love and to show mercy. Does this mean we are to reject our family members? No, Jesus was not saying we should dismiss them, and he chastised the Pharisees for not caring for their parents while they hypocritically preached the commandment to honor father and mother (Mark 7:9–13). Rather we honor all people, especially those in our care—fathers and mothers, children whom he blessed and compared to God's Empire (Mark 10:13–16), and "the least of these who are members of my family" (Matt 25:40).

So where do we draw the line between caring for family members, on the one hand, and letting go of them for the sake of God's will, on the other hand? It seems to me we draw the line where caring for our kinfolk becomes enabling them to behave badly, encouraging entitlement, or making them dependent beyond what is healthy for them. We do spare the rod but don't spoil the child so that he or she does not grow up feeling entitled to special privileges.[4]

A man I know grew up desperately needing the love of his absentee father who divorced his mother when he was a child. When my friend married and had a child of his own he transferred that need for love to his daughter and pampered her constantly, rescuing her from consequences of her bad behavior and in so doing teaching her to be dependent on him for constant bailouts and enabling her attitude of entitlement. Years went by as she turned to drug abuse, went to mental institutions, and finally rehab centers. My friend eventually got counseling himself, and gradually realized that his excessive need for love that drove him to please his daughter at any cost had actually crippled her psychologically so that she took too many years to grow up and learn to take care of herself. He has since worked hard to "cut the cord" and release his daughter from his needy love, thus freeing her to become a responsible adult.

This is a twenty-first century, psychological way of saying that healthy relationships empower our daughters, sons, brothers, sisters, and mothers to live out God's Empire of love, mercy, and fullness of life. These are our true kinfolks—those who do God's will by becoming loving, responsible adults.

4. Although the saying "spare the rod and spoil the child" is not in the Bible, Proverbs 13:24 does say, "Those who spare the rod hate their children, but those who love them are diligent to discipline them."

37

Getting a Life

"Those who try to make their life secure will lose it,
but those who lose their life will keep it."

(Luke 17:33–37; also Luke 9:24; Mark 8:35–36;
Matt 10:39; 16:25; and John 12:25)

"Remember Lot's wife. Those who try to make their life secure will lose it, but those who lose their life will keep it. I tell you, on that night there will be two in one bed; one will be taken and the other left. There will be two women grinding meal together; one will be taken and the other left." Then they asked him, "Where, Lord?" He said to them, "Where the corpse is, there the vultures will gather."

THERE ARE SIX VERSIONS of this wisdom saying of Jesus in the four canonical gospels. They are similar in their wording but quite different in their contexts. Yet, in every case the saying is a logical contradiction, a confusing paradox, and great material for a Monty Python mockery of biblical gibberish. Logically, a person either lives or does not live. Period. However, logic is not the Bible's strong suit or prime intent. So we have to take a look at how this saying fits into Jesus' whole message. We can make sense of it if we take account of the economic and political context of this saying.

Of the six versions of this saying, scholars have rated Luke 17:33 as closest to what Jesus may have said because the other five versions have words and phrases that suggest later additions and editing during the early church period when the cross became a focal symbol for the Jewish sect that became "Christian" decades after the crucifixion of Jesus.

This saying in Luke 17:33 is placed in an apocalyptic context when God's judgment was to come down like the destruction of Sodom, and Lot's wife looked back to her eternal regret. Likewise, at judgment day the eagles will gather where there is a corpse. As noted above, in this passage about eagles or vultures gathering (or being gathered), "eagles" could be a code word for Roman armies who are associated with death—either as killers or as those killed in God's judgment.

If this line of thinking—that Jesus was quite aware of Roman atrocities and spoke about them in coded language in the gospels—is right, then this saying about finding one's life can also be unpacked with this same assumption in mind. If we do so, we can observe that making "life secure" in occupied Palestine was to settle for and accept the political and economic conditions of exploitation set up by the Roman conquest. Those conditions, as we have noted, meant poverty and hopelessness for 95 percent of the people, and daily humiliation, ruthless torture, and death for those who resisted.

Being secure under these conditions was demanded of the other five percent who were made to cooperate with their occupiers of this conquered colony. However, those local leaders who cooperated exploited their own people in the hope that they could be secure themselves. Jesus' attitude toward that group of leaders was clear. He blasted them over and over. For example, lawyers and Pharisees might be considered secure, but Jesus says: "Woe also to you lawyers! For you load people with burdens hard to bear, and you yourselves do not lift a finger to ease them" (Luke 11:46). This woe or curse follows a long attack on the other "secure" group, Pharisees, whom he calls "fools," "full of greed and wickedness" (Luke 11:39–40). They "tithe mint and rue and herbs of all kinds, and neglect justice and the love of God" (Luke 11:42). Jesus hurled his "woes" at this tiny fraction of the people's leaders who may have had some relative security, because that security was based on the whims of their conquerors and the abuse of the 95 percent of their own people.

It makes sense to infer that in this paradoxical saying these lawyers and Pharisees are the ones who surrendered the righteous life of God's Empire for the tentative security of this colonial economic/political system. And those who will gain their life are those who "lose" or resist this system of corruption and death and will thereby gain their lives in the Empire of God's justice, which is Jesus' view of the true life.

To take a modern example: during WWII, to gain this corrupt security as the collaborators did with their Nazi conquerors in France was to lose the true life of God's love, equity, and goodness. But to lose the corrupt life by resisting Nazi (or Roman) rule was to gain the real life of God's love.

We can observe in the other five renderings of this saying besides Luke's that such an insecure life of resistance to oppression was like a cross to bear and that it may even lead to one's own physical death. But Jesus set the example of such resistance, as have martyrs ever since. Some things like God's justice are worth risking one's life for.

A recent example of risking one's supposedly secure life and gaining real life was pointed out to me in Prague, the Czech Republic. The head of biblical studies at Charles University gave me a tour of the significant monuments of Czech resistance. Professor Petr Pokorny walked me around the city to Bethlehem Chapel where John Hus preached resistance in the fifteenth century, a hundred years before Luther did so. He was burned at the stake in July 6, 1415 for his resistance but is honored with huge monuments in Prague today.

We also stopped at a bronze sculpture of eight student hands held up, most gesturing the "V" sign with their index and second fingers. This event was the beginning of the "Velvet Revolution" on November 17, 1989 (the date inscribed in bronze beneath the hands). My host pointed out although all the students' hands were unarmed, nevertheless, while demonstrating against the repressive government policies, the students were trapped in a street level enclosure and viciously beaten by police. This violent attack on unarmed students led to more and larger demonstrations and strikes. After only a few weeks, the Communist government collapsed like others in the eastern European countries that year. As I studied the monument, Professor Pokorny proudly mentioned that his daughter was one of the students in that demonstration that led to the democratically elected government of President Vaclav Havel and a new life for the Czech people.

For me, these students risking their lives and security to gain a new life free of a repressive government is an example of this wisdom saying. Those who lose their life (of secure oppression) will gain their life of free choice and government by the people. And the Czech people resisted non-violently, as did most of the eastern European demonstrators who won their freedom from Communist rule in 1989. That includes Hungary, East Germany, Poland, Yugoslavia, and Bulgaria. Romania was the only violent exception, for the Communist president and his wife were killed there.

It is rarely acknowledged, but nonviolence works. Jesus, the nonviolent radical, knew what he was talking about. So I connected these student hands of the Velvet Revolution, Hus at the stake, and Jesus on the cross (and their dates) in this sculpture as examples of those who risk their lives and in so doing gain them.

Gaining a Life

38

Shopping

"For where your treasure is, there will your heart will be also."
(Luke 12:32–34; also Matt 6:21; Gos Thom. 76)

> "Do not be afraid, little flock, for it is your Father's good pleasure to give you the kingdom. Sell your possessions, and give alms. Make purses for yourselves that do not wear out, an unfailing treasure in heaven, where no thief comes near and no moth destroys. For where your treasure is, there your heart will be also."

I ALWAYS THOUGHT THAT everyone else had my view of private property, ownership, possessions, and treasures until I got shocked out of my view and realized how narrow it was. But first, let us look at the text.

The three places where this saying appears (in Luke, Matthew, and Thomas) have in common the context of treasures, possessions, ownership, and personal property that insects can destroy. These treasures are compared to God's Empire, which is indestructible. Matthew and Luke add that a robber can steal possessions while Thomas attaches the saying to the priceless pearl parable.

The treasure of God's Empire is by far more worthy than all vulnerable possessions, priceless pearls, or any earthly treasures. If we give great worth to a thing or a person, our heart belongs to it. That is, we worship it. This is contrasted to the central call of the whole Bible and the first commandment to worship God alone.

This is fairly abstract theology, but it gets very concrete each day of our lives when we shop for things and interact with people. I have been taught and always assumed that my possessions were mine and I must take care of them. I thought private property was a universal principle that everybody, except maybe a few unenlightened people, took for granted. Then I learned from native people a whole different perspective on possessions, ownership, private property, and treasures.

I was on a trip with a native Hawaiian friend and was unprepared for a sudden change in the weather. I had dressed for summer temperatures but the weather got very cold and I needed warmer clothing. My friend, Kekapa Lee, a native Hawaiian, offered his jacket to me. It was a new and rather expensive one. I took the offer to be a brief loan until I warmed up. I had never imagined anyone giving away things that denied the owner's comfort, except perhaps a parent or maybe another close relative. But my imagination expanded the more I learned of native people and their very different concept of possessions. When we parted, I took off the jacket to return it to Kekapa Lee, but he insisted I must keep it. For this loaned jacket was his gift for me to keep. That was the Hawaiian way.

I began to see how I had always thought of ownership of my possessions as absolute. If I bought something, it was mine. Period. It was my responsibility to keep and protect it. Yet this gift of the jacket that I still wear after many years began to teach me that my culture's view of ownership and possessions is relative, not universal, and is even selfish.

However, Kekapa's generosity did not cause me to make a radical change in my view of private property at that time. It took much more contact with native people to alter my deeply ingrained perspective of ownership, possessions, private property, and my earthly treasures.

I periodically "teach" in a Lakota learning center on the Cheyenne River Reservation in South Dakota. I put "teach" in quotation marks because I learn as much or more from the Lakota pastors and future pastors when I go there as they learn from me. At a recent session I was given another gift, a bolo tie made of hundreds of tiny beads, which I was told had taken many hours to make. Later one of the native pastors complemented this bolo tie that I was wearing. I thanked him and went on "teaching." Soon after I learned that I had made a big mistake. It is the custom among the Lakota people to give away an object that is complimented. Yet following my own custom, I simply kept the gift tie as my own private property, my treasure. But now I was in "Indian Country" and needed to act appropriately—that is, to follow the native practice of the giveaway.

The giveaway is a frequent ceremony in which native people give away their possessions more formally than the occasions mentioned above. I recall a powwow in North Dakota at Sitting Bull College when another friend of mine was given a very elaborate war bonnet full of feathers and beads that covered his head and back almost to the ground. The giver was a Mandan from the Fort Berthold Reservation. If my culture had put a price on it, it would be in the thousands of dollars. But the giver did not think about pricing. The worth or value is judged differently. It had no price. It was a gift to give away and to honor the receiver.

Compare these formal and informal giveaway practices with our usual western consumer culture, and the difference is striking. We are endlessly assaulted with commercials to buy and to own massive quantities of objects we do not need, cannot afford, and have no place to put except perhaps in a self storage unit. Such storage facilities are springing up in almost every community to handle all this stuff we buy and store. Rather than give away our things, our treasures, we keep and store them for ourselves, even if we do not need them and never use them. And we shop. We often smile at the saying, "Shop 'til you drop." But it is a serious addiction for many people who "max out" their credit cards until they are bankrupt. To be sure, we need to shop for some necessary items. But we rarely ask ourselves if we are shopping for our needs or for our wants. Few people know that there really is another way than consumerism and shopping for useless wants. That other way is one that native people have perfected over thousands of years by giving away their possessions. Of course, they have had to adapt to some western ways to survive. But the native people I have known still try to practice giveaways to honor others by giving away their possessions on many occasions and even at funerals where gifts go to their ancestors in the spirit world. They have not assumed that private property is a high value. They do not think we can own the air we breathe, the water we drink, or indeed, even the land that we westerners guard with our ownership titles and our guns.

There is another way, one that is kinder to Mother Earth and to other people. It is strangely similar to the ancient wisdom of not laying up treasures on earth that insects destroy and robbers break in and steal. For "where your treasure is, there will your heart be also."

Shopping vs. Giving

I modeled this sculpture with a small person in the upper left corner overloaded with the shopper's packages. The woman at the center is also loaded with more stuff and has a posture and expression of entitlement. By contrast the native woman in the bottom right is carrying all her worldly goods on a horse drawn sled, which she might give away. Native people can teach us a lot about Jesus' wisdom.

39

Whom to Trust

"You will know them by their fruits."

(Matt 7:16; also Matt 12:33; Luke 6:43–45; Gos. Thom. 45)

"Beware of false prophets, who come to you in sheep's clothing but inwardly are ravenous wolves. You will know them by their fruits. Are grapes gathered from thorns, or figs from thistles? In the same way, every good tree bears good fruit, but the bad tree bears bad fruit. A good tree cannot bear bad fruit, nor can a bad tree bear good fruit. Every tree that does not bear good fruit is cut down and thrown into the fire. Thus you will know them by their fruits."

(Matt 7:15–20)

CERTAINLY HE COULD BE trusted, my friend assumed, for such a beautiful man must also manifest the other virtues of truth and goodness. Not that she was so philosophical after falling in love, but he seemed to have it all, and she was bowled over by him. He seemed the answer to all her prayers and then some. She was not financially secure and her house on which she owed more than it was worth needed much repair.

We start life as babies with this basic issue of trust or mistrust, according to famed psychologist Erik Erikson.[1] To trust or not to trust, that is the question, and it continues throughout our lives. Who among us has not been betrayed by someone we trusted? And who of us has not

1. Erikson, *Childhood and Society*, 219–22.

searched for trustworthy people, organizations, and even cars and other mechanical and natural objects that should do what they promise to do? We trust banks and the media (more or less) to keep our money safe and to tell the truth. We even trust politicians to govern with our best interests in mind, although we are frequently disappointed. Nevertheless, trust or the lack of trust is a central issue in living. Does Jesus' wisdom help us decide whom to trust?

Each day of our lives we count on ever so many people and things to be and behave in expected ways so we can do what we have to do. We count on doors to open, the car to run, and friends to love us and do what they say they will do. So how do we decide on whom we can count and on whom we *cannot* count? What does Jesus say?

Matthew, Luke, and Thomas each record this saying, though each frames it differently and Matthew repeats it in 12:33. All three gospels quote Jesus' image of grapes that are not grown from thorn bushes and of figs not grown from thistles or brambles. You can trust grapes to grow from grapevines and figs to grow from fig trees and not from other plants, let alone from thistles. Matthew's Jesus makes this image into an absurd question of grapes and figs growing from other plants. He also precedes it with a warning against trusting false prophets and adds that trees bearing bad fruit are cut down and thrown into the fire. Luke and Thomas do not have this typical condemnation of Matthew, but all three emphasize that trustworthiness comes from concrete behavior just as good fruit comes from good trees.

It is always good to ask, "as opposed to what?" Good trees and good people produce good fruit and vice versa. But we can best trust someone by seeing what they actually do and have done rather than what they *say* they will do, what they look like, how they dress, or what personal manners they display. Asking what someone has done in the past is the best way to determine how trustworthy people will be in the future.

Since all of our commerce and exchanges with other people count on some degree of trust, we are forced almost daily to judge whom to trust or not to trust. Hence, this issue of trust requires of us the best wisdom we can obtain. Jesus' wisdom implies other common sayings: "Don't judge a book by its cover." "Beauty is only skin deep." And, "The proof of the pudding is in the eating."

My friend fell madly in love with this handsome man she met at a party. He was everything she was not but everything she wanted, especially money. He had his own business as a licensed architect. And he was semi-available. That is, he was getting a divorce very soon and supposedly would have a very lucrative settlement including a (so-called) trust fund with plenty of money for his son's college expenses. This was to come from his very rich, soon-to-be ex-wife. His social skills were exceptional and he fit right in with her relatives. She could not imagine how lucky she was to have such a wonderful man in her life. And he offered his architectural skills to her.

He redesigned her house for her and hired workers to make many great improvements once the old furniture, walls, plumbing and electrical systems could be torn out. With his clever architectural design and her good credit rating, she was able to get a construction loan for these improvements and was delighted that she was getting all his architectural knowledge and skills free of charge. He was a gift from heaven she thought, until . . .

Until his divorce settlement dragged on for many months and, when it came, he and his ex-wife had no money left after paying off their divorce lawyers. The man and my friend began to argue in the empty construction site she had called home. The arguments became fights after she learned of his past relations with other women he had used and abandoned. They finally split up and she was left with a high interest loan debt, a wrecked house, and loneliness. She had trusted the man on the basis of his appearance and promises of a rich future in a beautiful, rebuilt house. She had not considered what he had done and not done; she had not considered the fruit of his labor.

This is a private story of trust betrayed when my friend did not follow Jesus' wisdom of knowing a person by what he had produced in the past (his fruit), rather than by what he promised for the future. The same wisdom applies to public issues in which larger numbers of people are involved, people both in our time and in Jesus' time.

When John the Baptist, whom Herod Antipas had imprisoned before he executed him, asked who Jesus was, Jesus did not respond by claiming his authority. Jesus did not respond with claims of privilege, status, legacy, royal lineage, or academic degrees. Rather, he identified who he was by *what he did and was doing*. He said to "tell John what you hear and see: the blind receive their sight, the lame walk, the lepers are cleansed, the deaf hear, the dead are raised, and the poor have good news brought to them" (Matt 11:2–7; also Luke 7:18–22). Then Jesus praised John by contrasting him to those who wear soft robes . . . in royal palaces" (Matt 11:8; also Luke 7:25), such as Herod Antipas. He then confronted the crowd with the question of why they listened to John in the first place. John is no "reed shaken in the wind." Of course not. John is the greatest person ever born but, even then, he is least in God's Empire. But that Empire is suffering violence now and the violent try to take it by force. (Again, that would be Rome, of course.) Then Jesus told a parable that ends with the equivalent of this wisdom saying: "You will know them by their fruits." He ends the parable with "Wisdom is vindicated by her deeds" (Matt 11:19).[2]

Known by Their Fruit

My friend (on the left) is flabbergasted that this wonderful man (on the right) whom she had trusted turned out to be untrustworthy. They stand in her house that is gutted and he, though nattily dressed, gives a helpless gesture and expression. She has learned the hard way to trust persons by their fruit, their deeds, not by what they promise.

2. Luke has the same parable of the Children in the Marketplace but ends it with "Wisdom is justified by her children" (7:35).

40

Money

"You cannot serve God and wealth."

(Matt 6:24; also Luke 16:13; Gos. Thom. 47b)

"No one can serve two masters; for a slave will either hate the one and love the other, or be devoted to the one and despise the other. You cannot serve God and wealth."

My friend Robert was the son of the president and CEO of a big bank in Texas who planned on Robert following him into the financial world. This projection of Robert's career started early, and by the time he had graduated from college with an economics major and had worked in his father's bank during school breaks, Robert's future seemed determined. But that was before he heard a seminary professor teach a course on the gospels that included this passage on the impossibility of serving both God and money.

The professor began in his lecture series at Robert's church observing that the gospels do not always agree exactly with each other on what Jesus said. Matthew says, "*No one* can serve two masters," and Luke says, "*No servant* can serve two masters." Both say, "You cannot serve God and wealth." The non-canonical Gospel of Thomas does not have the last phrase about God and money, and this is unusual because Thomas was frequently critical of merchants and businessmen. Perhaps Thomas simply assumed that the two masters were God and money, for he speaks of the difference so often elsewhere.

However, this wisdom saying could not be clearer, the professor said. It is a stark either/or choice, God *or* money. There is no both/and.

The service to one or the other means holding either God or money to be the highest value and giving one's energy, time, and commitment to one *or* the other. You simply cannot do both because there is no energy, time, or commitment left over for that. The professor called it a "zero sum" choice. Serving one means not only not serving the other but "despising" the other, as Matthew and Luke's Jesus says.

This has been interpreted as a personal and private warning against the "greed is good" belief of Gordon Geeko in the film *Wall Street* and against the other individual "Masters of the Universe" who gambled away other people's money and made millions for themselves in the great recession and then had their banks and investment companies bailed out with taxpayers' money.

Certainly Jesus' wisdom considers such private greed to be unethical. However, serving God or money is more than private ethics. Here is why, the professor explained: If we understand Jesus' society and our own as an economic/political system that is rigged to support a small, privileged group of people at the expense of all other people, then this saying is much more than a challenge to private greed or a personal choice of worshipping God or money.

This broader economic/political view requires us to "unrig" the whole economic/political system so that it serves everybody, not only the privileged few. The professor said he believed that serving God means just that. And as extravagant as it may seem, that means changing the whole, gigantic system. For Jesus said many times that we love God by serving our neighbors, especially those most in need (Matt 25:31–46; Luke 4:18). When we serve the poor, sick, hungry, imprisoned, and the least of these, and when we liberate the oppressed, then we serve the human one who is anointed to be God's agent. That is what the terms "Messiah" and "Christ" literally mean: the one who is confirmed by God to represent God. Jesus the Christ means the human being that God appointed as God's representative to carry out God's purposes.

The professor then asked, "What was the context of this saying?" This becomes blatantly clear when we discover that in Jesus' time it was *the Roman emperor* who claimed to be the only one who was anointed by the gods to be their earthly agent.

The trouble is that the emperor's gods did not want him to serve the poor, visit the sick, feed the hungry, release the imprisoned, or liberate the oppressed. The Roman gods ordained the emperor to protect and maintain the current ruling economic/political system of "eternal Rome," the Roman Peace. That was the system, the economic structure that was rigged in favor of the privileged few.

Thus, when we repeat Jesus' wisdom that we cannot serve God and money, we are saying that we cannot worship God and at the same time act with personal financial greed *or* support a system that benefits only the privileged few.

The professor acknowledged that our present day economic structure is much more complicated, that we do have a middle class in industrial nations that did not exist in Jesus' time, and that we all must earn money by which to live. But he drew the line between making money to live by and making money into a god we worship even if that harms other people or the environment.

Robert was torn apart spiritually after hearing this series of lectures. He began thinking about studying for the ministry even though other life plans had been clear and set for the future. Also, he was engaged to a Dallas debutante, and all his friends were well-off sons and daughters of wealthy oil and banking families. Even his church and its pastors were privileged to minister to the needs of the wealthy church members. Any criticism of the economic system within Robert's social network was immediately demonized with names such as "Socialism" or "Communism." He certainly would be shunned by his friends and would scare off his fiancée with his decision to go to seminary. But this opposition to his career change would pale in comparison to the rage he expected from his father.

And he got it . . . a full blast with an ultimatum of cutting off his inheritance and disowning him completely if Robert abandoned the plan to follow his father into a banking career. But Robert felt he had to go in another direction, and his economics education made him aware of these structural problems of economic systems. So he decided to go to seminary and pay the price.

But after three years of theology study and practice interning as a student pastor in a local church, he was still not satisfied with pastoral ministry. Robert felt that he could not minister only to the private needs of parishioners as a pastor is expected to do. Instead, Robert felt called to work at changing the system in which the rich get richer and the poor get poorer. He distinguished private ethics of greed from the evils of a rigged economic system. When he tried to explain this to his fiancée, she simply could not imagine being the spouse of a poor "social worker," the only occupation she could think of when Robert tried to describe what he wanted to do. She could not see herself with Robert in the poor, mostly black, section of Dallas where he would go. She thought only to lock her car doors when she occasionally passed through the area. But being shunned by her wealthy friends was the final possibility that she could not accept. So she broke off their engagement.

Robert kept at his effort to deal with the structural economic issues that kept people in perpetual poverty, as daunting as that was. He was determined to do what one person working with others could do to change the system in a few impoverished areas. So he became a community organizer in an inner city parish and is still working with impoverished people to resist exploitation. He could have chosen money but that would have cancelled out this serving the "least of these" in whom he finds the anointed agent of God.

Choose God or Money

41

Worry

"Do not fret. . . ."

(Gos. Thom. 36; also, Luke 12: 22–31; Matt 6:25–34)

"Do not fret, from morning to evening and from evening to morning, [about your food—what you are going to eat or about your clothing—what you are going to wear.] You are much better than the lilies, which neither card nor spin. As for you, when you have no garment, what will you put on? Who might add to your stature? That very one will give you your garment."

(Gos. Thom. 36)

When our church decided to become better stewards of the environment and install a solar electric system so we could get most of our energy free from the sun instead of from a coal-fired generating plant, we did not expect the opposition we got from our neighbors. We wanted to do our part to reduce global warming. But getting past the town Shade Tree Commission in Princeton, New Jersey quickly made us start to worry.

Jesus' wisdom is very clear about the uselessness of worry. And there is a variety of gospel reports on this saying about fretting or worrying. This saying suggests how similar but also how different the gospels are in reporting Jesus' wisdom sayings. The general point is: do not worry or fret about your daily cares such as food and clothing. The similarities between Matthew and Luke's versions are such that scholars agree they are from an earlier source they named "Q" from *Quelle*, the German word for "source."

However, Matthew puts this saying in the Sermon on the Mount, and Luke puts it right after the parable of the greedy, rich fool, probably to warn against such greed. Thomas has the simplest and most direct way of reporting Jesus' wisdom on worry: "Do not fret."

These different versions of the saying between the earlier Greek version of Thomas which is about worry over food and the later Coptic version about worry over clothing illustrates how variable the record is of what Jesus actually said. Thus, literal interpretations of the Bible make no sense. Putting Jesus' wisdom sayings in the broader context of the various gospels helps us to avoid literalism and to get a truer view of his real meaning. I think that the meaning is: worry is not useful and adds nothing to your life. This applies to each of us as individuals, but it has economic and political meaning as well.

This book applies Jesus' wisdom not only to individuals but also to the broader political/economic context of Jesus' time and our time. Our church's worry over installing the solar electric system in our church lasted over a year and led to excessive efforts to counter our neighbors' arguments and tactics of obstruction. We had a large pin oak tree that had to come down as it would block the sun from the solar panels on our church roof. The most active neighbor found argument after argument against taking down the tree such as that doing so would ruin her "viewscape," and the tree was simply a wonderful specimen. She arranged a botanist to come to the town council hearing and to argue for the need to keep the tree that helped reduce carbon, she said. We pointed out that the solar electric system would provide what amounted to five acres of trees like the pin oak and that we were going to plant even more trees elsewhere to replace the one we would take down.

But we continued to worry because the government rebate on which we were banking would expire a week after the town council met. We worried especially when the tree cutting company refused to cut the tree because a neighbor had secretly attached a sign to it warning of legal action if it were cut. But at the last minute before the rebate expired, we got tentative approval to proceed with the project and the tree cutting. Our pastor then had the bright idea of saving a tree sample to be analyzed at the state agricultural college. It turned out that the Pin Oak had a contagious disease and would have needed to come down in any case.

All our worry was for naught. A whole year of fretting over our neighbors' obstructions need not have happened. All that worry was useless, and it weighed us down needlessly.

Worry begins, of course, in our individual psyches as well as building up in a collection of people like our church. A private example of useless worry is when I fretted that I would sleep late and miss my plane to Chicago and an all-important, career-changing job interview. I got up early but worried that my car would not start on that cold morning. Then I worried about traffic on the way to Newark airport. I worried about parking, about making it through security, and that maybe the flight would be late or cancelled. When I got on board, I worried about a hijacking, and when we landed in Chicago, I fretted about the airport limousine getting trapped in a traffic pileup.

But when I got to the building at which I was to be interviewed, no one was there. I checked my watch ten times and confirmed that I had made it on time after all, even with a few minutes to spare. I was near panic with worry that I had mixed up the wrong day or the wrong week. How could I have gotten everything so wrong?

Finally, I looked up at a clock on the wall and saw that it was an hour earlier than my watch. I had forgotten that Chicago was on Central Time while my watch was on Eastern Time where I live. I had arrived an hour early and then some. My useless worry had nearly exhausted me. I waited an extra hour for the interview that turned out ok. But I had wasted all that energy with my worry.

In the image below, the diseased tree in the image on the left represents our church's worry. The clock represents my private fretting about being late. The incised figure with dagger in the upper right is the demon worry that haunts us uselessly.

Fret Not.

42

Asking for Help

"Ask, and it will be given you."

(Matt 7:7–11; also, Luke 11:9–13; John 5: 1–18; Gos. Thom. 2, 92, 94)

"Ask, and it will be given you; search and you will find; knock, and the door will be opened for you. For everyone who asks receives, and everyone who searches finds, and for everyone who knocks, the door will be opened. Is there anyone among you who, if your child asks for bread, will give a stone? Or if the child asks for a fish, will give a snake? If you then, who are evil, know how to give good gifts to your children, how much more will your father in heaven give good things to those who ask him?"

I ALWAYS DREADED SEPTEMBER because it was the back-to-school month and I was not good at school. I could get by ok in everything but reading, writing, and arithmetic. When I read books, I was so slow I rarely finished one. When I wrote an assigned essay, it was full of misspelled and even missing words. Arithmetic or mathematics was especially difficult because the numbers on the page, like letters and words in my reading and writing, reversed themselves, so that 56 would look like 65 and "was" would look like "saw." I thought I was really dumb. But I managed well on some tests such as multiple-choice quizzes when I only had to choose among a few given answers. I did ok in sports and got along with other students. My best and easiest learning was in pictures. I could easily identify images and spent much of class time drawing pictures rather than writing notes. The way I managed to learn literature, social studies, and, later on, philosophy and theology was to make graphs and images of the material to be learned.

I was very ashamed of my weakness in the 3 R's, and I hid this weakness like a bad criminal record. I would never reveal my problem to anyone, let alone ask for help. I was too proud for that. I tried to compensate by drawing and thinking in images, though I did not take a formal art course until I had almost finished graduate school. That was also the time when I read about a "learning disability" and began my search for what was wrong with me.

In this chapter, we look at Jesus' wisdom saying on asking for help. The usual interpretation of this saying is that God gives you what you ask for, as in a prayer request. But, of course, this does not always work. The focus has been on what you are *given* rather than on *if* and *how* you ask—that is, what *God* does or does not deliver rather than on *our* asking, seeking, and knocking. Another way to look at this saying is to ask the text, "as opposed to what?"

Asking, seeking, and knocking are obviously opposed to *not* asking, seeking, and knocking—that is, expecting a blessing without asking for it. When we do not *ask* but instead expect or wish for a blessing or favor, we assume we are entitled to it and deserve it. So, for example, we may think: "I deserve good things because I am good. I should not even need to ask, seek, and knock to get it." The Gospel of John dramatizes this when it reports Jesus asking the lame man at the pool of Bethzatha, "Do you want to be made well?" (5:6). That question of *wanting* to be made well is critical because the lame man may not *want* to be healed. He had been at the pool thirty-eight years and, when asked, he gave the excuse that others always beat him to the pool when it was stirred up and apparently able to heal. Sometimes we do not want to be healed. Or, like me, we are too proud to ask for help. Jesus' wisdom requires us to want to be healed enough to ask, seek, and knock and to say so before the healing is given. We must do our part. For, to ask for something is to declare ourselves, to state our own needs and affirm our vulnerable condition. That implies an obligation to do what we need to do to get well.

How often have children whined and cried for something and indulgent parents rushed to grant their desire even before the child *asked* for it? In Matthew, Jesus asks the question: When a child asks for bread or a fish, who would give the child a stone or snake (7:9–10)? This is clear enough.

But it is easy to overlook the fact that in this question the child *does ask*. This is compared to the child whining and crying and getting its way without requesting the bread or fish. (Luke makes the same point with bread or egg asked for and a stone or scorpion not given in 11:11–12.)

In the Alcoholics Anonymous' twelve-step program, one cannot begin the first step until one declares that one is powerless to help oneself. This first step requires an alcoholic to overcome pride and to ask for help. In step one a person says, "I am totally vulnerable and need help."

Jesus was affirming what every counselor knows: you cannot help a person who does not want to be helped and does not let that want be known by *asking* to be helped. By asking for help we declare that we are in need and that we will accept the help that is given, as opposed to hinting and assuming that the help is deserved or magically given. By searching we are already on the way to finding the answer, as opposed to passively waiting for it. By knocking on a door, we imply that we want the door to open and we will accept what is there, as opposed to expecting a magical opening and a choice to accept or reject the treatment.

Matthew puts the saying in the context of a list of Jesus' teachings. It appears after a warning not to throw pearls before swine and before the Golden Rule. Luke puts this saying in the context of prayer, that is, after the Lord's Prayer and the parable of the Friend at Midnight, which Luke interprets as calling for persistence in prayer. Thomas scatters the saying about seeking and knocking in chapters 2, 93, and 94. There is no reference to asking in Thomas.

Ask and Receive

I learned how important it is to ask for help on my personal journey. My search for what was wrong with me regarding my learning disability led me to a new word, "dyslexia." The symptoms of dyslexia fit me perfectly. I could not spell. I reversed letters and numbers, and consequently found most tests very difficult. But I had hidden this problem for decades out of shame and fear of exposure. Finally, I put my shame aside enough to ask for help. I knocked on the door of a college psychology department where I could be tested for learning problems and discovered I was very dyslexic. The man who tested me was astonished that I had gotten through graduate school despite my learning problem.

I wish I had asked for help much sooner because there are exercises and other aids to help remediate dyslexia. I finally got the help I needed, but I did not ask, search, or knock on the right doors for the many years during which I struggled with my hidden problem. To be sure, the way I compensated was a hidden blessing that drove me to visual art. Yet, my refusal to want to be healed enough to ask, seek, and knock on the right doors made for years of dread, especially the dread of going back to school each September.

Jesus said, "Ask and it will be given you." We have to do our part.

This sculpture is in the Sanctuary of First Congregational Church, UCC in Boulder, Colorado where all people are welcome, even dyslexics.

43

Resisting Temptations

"The spirit indeed is willing but the flesh is weak".

(Mark 14:37b–38; also Matt 26:41b)

"Simon, are you sleeping? Could you not keep awake for one hour? Keep awake and pray that you may not come into the time of trial; the spirit indeed is willing, but the flesh is weak."

TOBIAS WAS A PASTOR with many talents. Storytelling was one of them, and he used this skill very effectively in his preaching. His congregations loved his sermons, and he was being considered for higher positions in his church hierarchy. He enjoyed his church work and the parishioners he served. They responded with very positive evaluations of his ministry because they liked him very much, too much perhaps in his last church. At least too much by Judy whose failing marriage led her to seek Tobias' advice and to temptations that he found hard to resist.

Before we examine what happened to them, let us look at how Jesus resisted temptations of a life and death sort.

One of the traits that is rarely noted about Jesus is his very strong willpower to resist temptation. Perhaps that is too obvious or perhaps it is unbelievable that he could resist temptations so great. But throughout the gospels he is tempted to forsake his mission; yet he never gives in. In the wilderness temptation, Satan tempted him with magical powers to make food, to defy gravity, to rule all the kingdoms of the world (Matt

4:1–10). His willpower resisted these temptations at the beginning of his ministry. He even resisted the appeals of his family to stop his risky behavior as people were saying he was out of his mind (Mark 3:21, 34–35). He refused to give up when his cousin, John the Baptist, was beheaded.

Finally, in the Garden of Gethsemane he resisted the temptation to give up the plan to challenge the whole power structure of Rome and its collaborators. He even prayed for God to relieve him of this deadly mission. But he judged it to be God's will and thus his own to go through with this challenge. So he willed himself to proceed and to face a sure sentence of death. Then he discovered that his disciples were lacking his strength of will. For he found them sleeping and said, "Couldn't you stay awake one hour? Be alert and pray that you won't be put to the test! The spirit is willing but the flesh is weak."

My friend Tobias had served a number of churches and was at the peak of his ministry. The big move for which he was being considered was one he desperately wanted. If he got it, that would carry him to a comfortable retirement. However, there was one big issue for him. He and his wife had marital problems and fought often and hard.

One evening after a difficult board meeting, he went home especially hungry, angry, lonely, and tired, and was surprised to find neither his wife nor food at home. He dealt with his frustration as he usually did, with more work. He went back to the church to do a final polishing of his Sunday sermon. On his way he grabbed a big sandwich and a bottle of wine. Then when he arrived at the church, he was surprised to find that Judy was there, crying. Her husband had come home after too many beers with his friends, though he had promised Judy he would stop drinking. She was livid at his broken promises and his out-of-control behavior. She told him so. He became threatening, so she left and sought help from her pastor, Tobias.

Both he and Judy were hungry, angry, lonely, and tired. Tobias knew from his counseling training that these conditions spelled out the anagram "HALT," (Hungry, Angry, Lonely, Tired), a warning that under those conditions one's willpower was usually weak and one's temptations strong. Tobias invited Judy to share his sandwich and wine in the pastor's study. After the meal and long conversations about their rocky marriages, the temptation to sleep together on the couch in his study was too much for them to resist. Thus, an affair began and continued for some weeks in "safer" locations. That night after a few hours of sleep on the couch in front of a picture of Jesus on the wall behind them (asking "could they not resist temptation?"), they departed for their separate homes. Their spouses eventually found out and told the congregation and the regional church authorities. Tobias had to leave the church, his marriage, and eventually, ministry itself.

I felt very sad for all involved in the situation. Blessedly, Tobias was old enough to start collecting his pension early, which he did not lose. And he eventually reconciled with his wife, though Judy divorced her husband. What Tobias has not yet reconciled is his relation to the church. He never attends any church now. He asked me the rhetorical question: "Why did I get such a raw deal from the church?" I did not try to answer. I thought his bitterness was still too great for him to know that he had been "put to the test," and to hear that God's forgiving grace is deep and wide and is his for the asking.

Of course, there are endless temptations that test our will power; though our spirit is willing to resist, our flesh is weak. It is so easy to abandon the way of Jesus and even common sense, and do crazy things that hurt ourselves and others. A recent article, "Pumping Up Self Control [Willpower] in an Age of Temptations," asks if we are weaker than our parents and grandparents in resisting temptations. The author quotes Professor Kathleen Vohs at Carlton School of Management: "There is research that shows people still have the same self-control as in decades past, but we are bombarded more and more with temptations . . . Our psychological system is not set up to deal with all the potential immediate gratification."[1] Vohs goes on to detail how we are constantly tempted, and describes how will power, like a muscle, can get fatigued if over used. Although the temptations will always be there, we do not have to act on them.

Other temptations besides sex abound and are too many to list here, but the epidemic of obesity demands at least brief attention. For most people in the U.S., our individual willpower is "put to the test" at every meal time, and much more now than in the past. Former Food and Drug Administration commissioner, David Kessler has tried to answer the question of why we are so obese. His answer goes beyond our private willpower noting that the food industry has "hijacked people's brains

1. Tugend, *New York Times*, October 9, 2010, B6.

with high fat, high sugar"[2] and high salt foods, and our brains are now conditioned to demand these fat-forming foods.

Whatever the temptations—sex, food, or other addictions—the economics of profit-making are partly responsible. Thus our individual will power must "keep awake and pray that [we] may not come into the time of trial." But we must also join with others to resist the economic power of big food corporations because we are "put to the test" more now than ever; and though our Spirit may be willing, our flesh is weak.

Temptations

2. "Researcher answers the weight gain question," Edward M. Eveld, *Trenton Times*, October 18, 2010, B7.

44

Adultery

"Who is without sin be the first to cast a stone."

(John 8:2–11)

Early in the morning he came again to the temple. All the people came to him and he sat down and began to teach them. The scribes and the Pharisees brought a woman who had been caught in adultery; and making her stand before all of them, they said to him, "Teacher, this woman was caught in the very act of committing adultery. Now in the law Moses commanded us to stone such women. Now what do you say?" They said this to test him, so that they might have some charge to bring against him. Jesus bent down and wrote with his finger on the ground. When they kept on questioning him, he straightened up and said to them, "Let anyone among you who is without sin be the first to throw a stone at her." And once again he bent down and wrote on the ground. When they heard it, they went away, one by one, beginning with the elders; and Jesus was left alone with the woman standing before him. Jesus straightened up and said to her, "Woman, where are they? Has no one condemned you?" She said, "No one, sir." And Jesus said, "Neither do I condemn you. Go your way, and from now on do not sin again."

The accusers of this woman are following part of the law stated in the First Testament, Deuteronomy 22:20–24, in which adulterers (both male and female) who are caught are stoned to death. Which ones are stoned depends on the marital status of the man and the woman. Two witnesses are required and a witness is the one to cast the first stone. The accusers in this story clearly wanted to set a trap for Jesus, putting him on the spot to either support or oppose Moses' law. But Jesus, while writing on the ground, plays it very cool and finally turns the tables on the accusers and says, "Let anyone among you who is without sin be the first to throw a stone at her." The accusers have to drop their stones, for who is without sin?

This sculpture is a fired clay model for a possible bronze cast to be set up at Eden Theological Seminary near St. Louis, Missouri. At least that was the original plan, but bronze is very expensive and the topic, though biblical, can be a problem. The plan is still pending.

This image is different from other classical images of this passage. First, I included the adulterous man in the upper right corner escaping the accusers, clothes and shoes in hand who, if caught, was also to be stoned according to Moses' law. Instead of the usual image in classical paintings of a shamed, older, and buxom woman, this woman is very young and terrified. On the left panel she is tied up and the accusers are ready with their stones.

The Accusers

On the right side are the accusers dropping the stones and the young woman, free of the ropes, is celebrating her release. Jesus is in the middle writing on the ground and offering to anyone who is without sin a stone to cast, including modern viewers. That is, he is offering the first stone to be cast, but only with the defining condition of that accuser's own sinlessness. This wisdom of Jesus suggests that adultery laws are clearly beyond the reach of law enforcement and do not warrant criminal, let alone capital, punishment, although this is not the case in some strict, Islamic countries where stoning is still sometimes practiced.

It also suggests that the paternalism assumed in punishing only the woman is not consistent with Jesus' teachings or with Mosaic Law. Jesus directly challenged the brutal mistreatment of women, showing great respect for women. Women were among his first followers, the last witnesses to his crucifixion, and the first witnesses to the resurrection.

On a more public level, the whole system of domination in biblical times required that women be exploited and controlled by a paternalism that kept them as virtual household slaves to men who alone had all of the public roles. Women could not even be public witnesses or hold public positions. Thus only the woman, not the adulterous man, is presented to Jesus for his judgment—an oppressive game he refused to play. Instead, John's Jesus challenged the whole patriarchal system with his wisdom saying: "Who is without sin be the first to cast a stone."

45

Seeing the Light

"The eye is the lamp of the body."

(Matt 6:22–23; also Luke 11:34–36)

"The eye is the lamp of the body. So, if your eye is healthy, your whole body will be full of light; but if your eye is unhealthy, your whole body will be full of darkness. If then the light in you is darkness, how great is the darkness!"

In Jesus' time there were no light bulbs, of course. The only light was from flames: lamps, torches, fires, and from the heavenly lights: sun, moon, and stars. So it is easy to see how, for people in the first century, light became a symbol for heavenly goodness and darkness a symbol for evil. In addition, people then believed that the eye channeled light into the body. They did not separate the physical (eye and body) from the spiritual (good and evil) as we do. So light is used throughout the Bible (194 times) as a word for goodness, especially in the Gospel of John (Twenty-two times, e.g.,"The light shines in the darkness, and the darkness did not overcome it," 1:5).

This saying is an abstract bit of wisdom that has many interpretations. I would like to focus on the notion that narrowness of vision or "tunnel vision," can be harmful. Such tunnel vision is symbolized with darkness. And openness of vision (seeing the light) can liberate us from that harmful darkness. Yet tunnel vision is not all bad. It is often necessary for great accomplishments, especially in learning and art. My personal experience in getting a Ph.D. was that it required my total focus, even a myopic, tunnel vision. I had to do virtually nothing else but read and write on a narrow subject to finish a dissertation for the degree.

I let go of great deal of daily life so I could finally get the thing written. But my infant son intervened at a very low point in my years of graduate study. I sent my dissertation off to my major professor and waited in existential dread for his response. It came back in a package in the mail. I took it into my diningroom table, sat down and slowly opened it.

Let me explain a bit more about what I mean about tunnel vision's being necessary for great accomplishments. The poet Rainer Maria Rilke did not participate in his daughter Ruth's wedding. He did not even attend it for fear he would lose his intense focus on his poetry.[1] Vincent van Gogh's enormous production of great art in only ten years is another example of the need for intense focus. His letters to his brother (*Dear Theo*) illustrate that laser beam attention to one thing, his painting.[2] When most of one's energy is focused on just one project, one manages to do little else. This is positive in that we have this great art and poetry. It is negative in that these geniuses missed so much else in life, especially human connections.

Unless we are geniuses like Rilke and van Gogh, the negative side of tunnel vision is that it rarely allows us to see ourselves and others wisely and fully. Without that wisdom, that broad vision, we can also limit ourselves to a rigid, constricted life of safety, comfort, and narrowness. Being so constricted, we think we cannot accomplish things, so we do not. With tunnel vision we often dismiss others with an easy, negative judgment. And we become blind to the beauty of God's creation, the tiny flower, and the magnificent night sky, although Rilke and van Gogh certainly were not blind to these; and their genius was that they could focus so intently yet find the beauty of all God's creation. But most of us can easily fall into parochialism, nationalism, and other narrow-minded views of the world with narrow vision.

Postcolonial writers are now helping us see that our western perspective is distorted with the narrow notion of western supremacy which assumes that the other two thirds of the world is backward and in need of our imperial culture. These assumptions are so deeply buried in western literature, such as the novel, that we cannot even see them. Hence, an early writer in this Postcolonial field, the late Edward W. Said,

1. Rilke, *Selected Poems of Rainer Maria Rilke*, 157.

2. Van Gogh, *Dear Theo: The Autobiography of Vincent Van Gogh*.

a Palestinian-American scholar, concluded: "Without empire, I would go so far as saying, there is no European novel as we know it."[3] He analyzes many writers, especially British novelists, such as Jane Austen, whose novels are omnipresent on our TV screens on Masterpiece Theater. Her 1814 novel, *Mansfield Park*, illustrates the given assumption of western superiority and imperial conquest as the Mansfield Park Manor is supported by profits from a sugar plantation in Antigua worked by slaves. (Slavery was not abolished in the British Empire until 1833.) Yet we read about and watch girls and women, manners and romances in Austen's novels as if this wretched background of imperialism and slavery were simply a normal, a given, the unchangeable way things are. Said declares that in her novels, Austen "reveals herself to be *assuming* . . . the importance of an empire to the situation at home . . . According to Austen we are to conclude that no matter how isolated and insulated the English place (e.g., Mansfield Park), it requires overseas sustenance."[4]

Postcolonial writers are now lifting up this imperial normalcy for all to see, revealing the darkness of empire that our western literature has ignored for centuries, just as theologians have ignored the imperialism of Rome by assuming that it was a normal and given, even acceptable, background to Jesus' time. We in the west must open our eyes to the devastation brought by colonists in the name of saving "the heathen." For if our eyes can see with this broader perspective, the light of goodness may find entry into our body politic.

This sculpture of Jane Austen shows her above the Mansfield Park mansion with a carriage carrying ladies to a tea while on the right side her arm—like Mansfield Park—leans on and is dependent on the torture of slaves in Antigua.[5]

3. Said, *Culture and Imperialism*, 69.

4. Ibid., 89.

5. On seeing a 1999 film adaptation by Patricia Rozema of *Mansfield Park*, one sees pictures of the atrocities of slavery depicted most graphically and they "horrif[y] the characters." But those clear references to slavery are not in the novel. Notes in the Barnes and Noble Classic edition of the novel by Amanda Claybaugh say that Austen "only alludes" to the slave trade; "in the novel Austen's characters never discuss such social issues" (416). The film version added these images that clearly condemn slavery which the novel did not.

Dependent on Slavery

Back to my personal focus on a dissertation at the expense of most everything else. Nearly all of my time, money, energy, and vision were focused there. At that moment when I opened the package from my professor, my life depended on a good review. By then I had a full-time job and no time to rework the dissertation. When I pulled out the three-inch high stack of papers, my heart sank. The sentences were full of red marks and the margins full of rejections. I got a very bad review. My dissertation was not acceptable. It had to be totally rewritten with major revisions. I had never sunk so low as this, then or since. My head fell on the table. My arm drooped down to the floor. Surely all the world, all my friends and relatives, would condemn and shame me for being such a failure. All seemed lost.

That was when I felt a very slimy round object easing into my drooping hand. Peaking down through my teary eyes, I saw the grinning face of my son who had just given me his squishy treasure, a wet ping pong ball. Moreover, to my great surprise, this infant child of mine did not seem to care what a useless failure he had for a father. That ping pong ball he pulled out of his mouth after finding it in his explorations beneath the chairs and table rescued me from my tunnel vision, and I learned to see a bigger picture that included this little gift giver and his loving acceptance of me.

I got over my depression, took a short sabbatical, rewrote the dissertation, asked my spouse, Carol, to retype it, and then defended it adequately after many months. My myopic vision was en-lightened and my eyes began to see through the loving eyes of my son. I can say, and know it is true, that my eyes saw the light of goodness that day.

This book and this DVD are all about the light of goodness we can see with expanded vision, an openness to visual images, and seeing the full context of Jesus' wisdom that includes the political and economic realities of his time and our own.

Conclusion

THIS BOOK IS AN effort to fill in a number of gaps in the usual way we teach and preach the Christian faith. The first gap is the lack of images that "speak" a visual language where the verbal and written languages have dominated. Of course, there are images in Sunday school material and countless stained glass windows and classic fine art in the cathedrals of Europe. But, like the need to translate biblical words for each generation, images need the same new translations where they exist. Sadly there still is a bias against images in churches and seminaries where the Word and words are clearly dominant. I have tried to show how the Word can also be expressed in images.

The second gap in interpreting Jesus' wisdom has been our lack of knowledge about the political and economic context of the Bible, particularly in the gospels, as well as our lack of knowledge about that context in our own time. That gap has existed through history until recently. But by acknowledging that the gospels, seen critically, have "hidden transcripts," or coded messages within a political and economic context of a poor and conquered people, the gospels come alive with amazing wisdom for us today.

Third, I have sought to begin filling the gap left by most scholars who do account for the political and economic context, with my interpretation of specific wisdom sayings. The majority of scholars who do acknowledge the political and economic context of the Bible give us helpful general theory, but leave us wondering about the specific sayings attributed to Jesus. I have started to fill this gap by assuming the theory and directly interpreting particular sayings. Pastors nearly always preach on a specific passage of scripture rather than on general theories about them.

Fourth, this is for pastors who need access every week to useful background on Jesus' wisdom that has stories and pictures to project for their sermons. The stories I have told here will, I hope, inspire others to tell their stories to illustrate Jesus' wisdom for us today. But it is also written for lay people using non-technical language as much as possible.

Fifth, this book can be used for short devotions in which a saying is examined quickly and as a whole. This approach makes the material adaptable for the little time left us for serious reflection in our busy lives. One can pick any saying in the book, read it, see a new image on the saying, and absorb its wisdom without a commitment to a long, single reading period.

Sixth, I have sought to fill a gap left by the lack of thoughtful and complex images of these sayings. I have created original sculptures that go beyond clichéd pictures and that reach the often hidden and coded voice of Jesus' first audience of people who were "like sheep without a shepherd" (Mark 6:34), "harassed and helpless" (Matt 9:36). The images here can be used in church newsletters, bulletins, posters, and other printed material, as well as projected in worship and education settings. Having an image or images on which a whole group may focus at the same time helps bind them to a central visual thought that provides immediate and long term community as well as communication. Since it was not possible to include the DVD in this book, please order it from the author at the address given previously. I give permission to reproduce images from the book and DVD for one time educational use if credit is given to me and no sales of them are made. Please send me a copy of your use of the images to cmccollough2@verizon.net and see my web site, www.sculpturebymccollough.com.

Seventh, I am leaving a gap myself to be filled later in that there are more wisdom sayings than I can visualize, sculpt, and interpret at this time. So I see this book and DVD as only a beginning effort but nonetheless a useful tool for learning, teaching, and preaching Jesus' wisdom, a tool that distinguishes between what we can and cannot change and thereby gives us both serenity toward the unchangeable and courage to follow the Nonviolent Radical in changing this world.

Bibliography

Acocella, Joan. *Twenty-eight Artists and Two Saints: Essays*. New York: Pantheon, 2007.

Berrigan, Daniel, and Margaret Parker. *Stations: The Way of the Cross*. San Francisco: Harper and Row, 1989.

Borg, Marcus J. *Meeting Jesus Again for the First Time*. New York: Harper, 1994.

Borg, Marcus J., and John Dominic Crossan. *The Last Week: A Day by Day Account of Jesus's Final Week in Jerusalem*. New York: Harper, 2006.

Bourgeault, Cynthia. *The Wisdom Jesus: Transforming Heart and Mind—A New Perspective on Christ and His Message*. Boston: Shambhala, 2008.

Brock, Rita Nakashima, and Rebecca Ann Parker. *Saving Paradise: How Christianity Traded Love of This World for Crucifixion and Empire*. Boston: Beacon, 2008.

Carter, Jimmy. *Talking Peace*. New York: Dutton, 1993.

Carter, Warren. "Are There Imperial Texts in the Class? Intertextual Eagles and Matthean Eschatology as 'Lights Out' Time for Imperial Rome (Matthew 24:27–31)." JBL 122/3 (2003) 467–87.

———. *John and Empire: Initial Explorations*. New York: T and T Clark, 2008.

———. *Matthew and Empire: Initial Explorations*. Harrisburg, PA: Trinity, 2001.

———. *The Roman Empire and the New Testament: An Essential Guide*. Nashville: Abingdon, 2006.

———. *What Does Revelation Reveal? Unlocking the Mystery*. Nashville: Abingdon, 2010.

Crossan, John Dominic. *The Birth of Christianity: Discovering What Happened in the Years Immediately After the Execution of Jesus*. San Francisco: Harper, 1998.

———. *The Essential Jesus: What Jesus Really Taught*. San Francisco: Harper, 1994.

———. *God and Empire: Jesus Against Rome, Then and Now*. San Francisco: Harper, 2007.

———. *The Greatest Prayer: Rediscovering the Revolutionary Message of the Lord's Prayer*. New York: HarperCollins, 2010.

———. *The Historical Jesus: The Life of a Mediterranean Jewish Peasant*. San Francisco: Harper, 1991.

———. *Jesus: A Revolutionary Biography*. San Francisco: Harper: 1995.

Crossan, John Domini, and Jonathan L. Reed. *In Search of Paul: How Jesus's Apostle Opposed Rome's Empire with God's Kingdom*. San Francisco: Harper, 2004.

Dube, Musa W, and Jeffrey L. Staley, eds. *John and Postcolonialism: Travel, Space and Power*. London: Sheffield, 2002.

Dudley, Donald R. *The Civilization of Rome*. New York: New American Library, 1960.

Ehrman, Bart D. *Misquoting Jesus: The Story Behind Who Changed the Bible and How*. San Francisco: Harper, 2005.

Elliott, Neil. *The Arrogance of Nations: Reading Romans in the Shadow of Empire*. Minneapolis: Fortress, 2010.

Frazier, Ian. *On the Rez*. New York: Farrar, Straus, Giroux, 2000.

Friedman, Donald. *The Writer's Brush: Paintings, Drawings and Sculpture by Writers.* Minneapolis: Midlist, 2007.

Funk, Robert W., and Roy W. Hoover. *The Five Gospels: The Search for the Authentic Words of Jesus.* New York: MacMillan, 1993.

Funk, Robert W., Bernard Brandon Scott, and James Butts. *The Parables of Jesus: Red Letter Edition.* Sonoma, CA: Polebridge, 1988.

Herzog, William R., II. *Prophet and Teacher: An Introduction to the Historical Jesus.* Louisville, KY: Westminster John Knox, 2005.

Horsley, Richard A. *Jesus and the Spiral of Violence: Popular Jewish Resistance in Roman Palestine.* San Francisco: Harper and Row, 1987.

———. *Jesus in Context: Power, People, and Performance.* Minneapolis: Fortress, 2008.

———. *In the Shadow of Empire: Reclaiming the Bible as a History of Faithful Resistance.* Louisville, KY: Westminster John Knox, 2008.

Jensen, Robin Margaret. *Face to Face: Portraits of the Divine in Early Christianity.* Minneapolis: Fortress, 2005.

———. *The Substance of Things Seen: Faith, Art, and the Christian Community.* Grand Rapids: Eerdmans, 2004.

———. *Understanding Early Christian Art.* New York: Routledge, 2000.

Josephus, Flavius. *Josephus: The Complete Works.* Translated by William Whiston. Nashville: Thomas Nelson, 1998.

Kapikian, Catherine. *Art in Service of the Sacred.* Edited by Kathy Black. Nashville: Abingdon, 2006.

Kautsky, John H. *The Politics of Aristocratic Empires.* New Brunswick, NJ: Transaction, 1997.

Keller, Catherine, Michael Nausner, and Mayra Rivera, eds. *Postcolonial Theologies: Divinity and Empire.* St. Louis: Chalice, 2004.

King, Martin Luther, Jr. *Strength to Love.* New York: Walker, 1963.

Krugman, Paul. "A Tale of Two Moralities." *New York Times*, January 14, 2011.

McKenzie, Alyce M. *Preaching Proverbs: Wisdom for the Pulpit.* Louisville, KY: Westminster John Knox, 1996.

Miles, Margaret R. *The Word Made Flesh: A History of Christian Thought.* Malden, MA: Blackwell, 2005.

Mitchell, George J. *Making Peace.* New York: Knopf, 1999.

Moore, Stephen D. *Empire and Apocalypse: Postcolonialism and the New Testament.* Sheffield, UK: Sheffield Phoenix, 2006.

Newsom, Carol A., and Sharon Ringe, eds. *Women's Bible Commentary.* Louisville, KY: Westminster John Knox, 1998.

Nichols, J. Randall. *Building the Word: The Dynamics of Communication and Preaching.* San Francisco: Harper and Row, 1980.

Oakes, Peter, ed. *Rome and the Early Church.* Grand Rapids: Baker, 2002.

Patterson, Stephen J. *Beyond the Passion: Rethinking the Death and Life of Jesus.* Minneapolis: Fortress, 2004.

———. *The God of Jesus: The Historical Jesus and the Search for Meaning.* Harrisburg, PA: Trinity, 1998.

Rilke, Rainer Maria. *Selected Poems of Rainer Maria Rilke.* Translation and commentary by Robert Bly. New York: Harper and Row, 1981.

Said, Edward W. *Culture and Imperialism.* New York: Vintage, 1994.

Sanford, John A. *The Kingdom Within: the Inner Meaning of Jesus' Sayings.* San Francisco: Harper, 1987.

Scott, James C. *Domination and the Arts of Resistance: Hidden Transcripts*. New Haven, CT: Yale University Press, 1990.

———. *Weapons of the Weak: Everyday Form of Peasant Resistance*. New Haven, CT: Yale University Press, 1985.

Segovia, Fernando F. *Decolonizing the Bible: A View from the Margins*. New York: Orbis, 2000.

Segovia, Fernando F., and Mary Ann Tolbert. *Reading from this Place: Social Location and Biblical Interpretation in the United States*. Vol. 1. Minneapolis. Fortress, 1995.

Sharp, Gene. *The Politics of Non-violent Action*. Boston: Porter Sargent, 1973.

Sugirtharajah, R. S., ed. *The Postcolonial Bible*. Sheffield, UK: Sheffield Academic, 1998.

———. *Postcolonial Criticism and Biblical Interpretation*. Oxford: Oxford University Press, 2002.

———. *Postcolonial Reconfigurations: An Alternative Way of Reading the Bible and Doing Theology*. St. Louis: Chalice, 2003.

———, ed. *Voices from the Margin: Interpreting the Bible in the Third World*. Maryknoll, NY: Orbis, 2006.

Troeger, Thomas H. *Above the Moon Earth Rises: Hymn Texts, Anthems, and Poems for the New Creation*. New York: Oxford University Press, 2002.

———. *Borrowed Light: Hymns Texts, Prayers and Poems*. New York: Oxford University Press, 1994.

Updike, John. "The Artist as Showman: A Conversation with John Updike." Interview by Bruce Cole. *Humanities* 29/3 (May/June, 2008) 6–9, 51–53.

———. *Just Looking: Essays on Art*. Boston: MFA Publications, 2001.

———. *Still Looking: Essays on American Art*. New York: Knopf, 2006.

Van Gogh, Vincent. *Dear Theo: The Autobiography of Vincent Van Gogh*. Edited by Irving Stone and Jean Stone. New York: Doubleday, 1937.

Vrudny, Kimberly, and Wilson Yates, eds. *Arts, Theology, and the Church: New Intersections*. Cleveland: Pilgrim, 2005.

Walls, Jeannette. *The Glass Castle*. New York: Scribner, 2005.